Transportation —

Mike
The life and times of Mike Hailwood

By the same author:

Hailwood
The Yamaha Legend
Mike the Bike – Again

Mike
The life and times of Mike Hailwood

TED MACAULEY

BUCHAN & ENRIGHT, PUBLISHERS
LONDON

First published in 1984 by
Buchan & Enright, Publishers, Ltd
53 Fleet Street, London EC4Y 1BE

Copyright © Ted Macauley 1984

All rights reserved. No part of this publication
may be reproduced, stored in a retrieval system,
or transmitted, in any form or by any means,
electronic, mechanical, photocopying, recording,
or otherwise, without the prior permission in
writing of the publishers.

British Library Cataloguing in Publication Data

Macauley, Ted
   Mike.
   1. Hailwood, Mike
   I. Title
   796.7'5'0924   GV1060.2.H26

ISBN 0-907675-22-0

Photoset in North Wales by
Derek Doyle & Associates, Mold, Clwyd
Printed in Great Britain by
Biddles Limited, Guildford

Contents

	Acknowledgements	6
1	Death of a Legend	11
2	Pauline's Story, and more ...	29
3	TT 1978	54
4	TT 1979	81
5	The Motor-Cycle Star	99
6	The Full Genius	127
7	Driving Forces	137
	Index	157

Acknowledgements

My grateful thanks for their help are due to: Giacomo Agostini, Mike Anslow, Dickie Attwood, Chris Bateman, Ralph Bryans, Chris Buckler (Mike's sister), John Cooper, Mick Grant, David Hobbs, John O'Dell, Phil Read, Rod Sawyer, Tom Wheatcroft, Steve Wynne, and Pauline.

I am grateful also to the following for help with the photographs: Adrian Ashurst, Chris Bateman, John Everett, the *Daily Mirror*, and Mick Woollett.

Illustrations

Following page 64

Stan Hailwood (*Chris Bateman*)
Mike with his sister Chris (*Chris Bateman*)
Ripping up the lawn at home
Competing in the 1957 Scottish Six Days Trial
On a Manx Norton in 1959 (*Mick Woollett*)
With Degner and Provini at the 1959 Dutch TT (*Mick Woollett*)
Mike with the 500 MV in 1961 (*Mick Woollett*)
Hailwood and Bill Ivy on the curling rink
The famous Honda 250-6 (*Völker Rauch*)
Phil Read on a Norton in 1963
With his step-mother after the court case (*Daily Mirror*)
Mike and the Lotus on their way to sixth at Monaco (*J.M. Ploton*)
The classic Hailwood style
With the battered MV 500 in the 1965 Senior
Hailwood follows Agostini in the 1965 East German GP
The evil-handling Honda 500-4 (*Features International*)
Mike with Honda team-mate Jim Redman
Hailwood in 1965 ... (*Völker Rauch*)
And two years later (*Völker Rauch*)

Following page 96

Giacomo Agostini on the MV 500-4
Mike and Stanley Woods in 1967
In BSA livery for Daytona
Winner of the Formula Two car championship (*Thomson Allied Newspapers*)
Mike in the Yardley-McLaren M23 during a GP (*Thomson Allied Newspapers*)
In hospital after the Nürburgring crash that ended his car-racing career (*Daily Mirror*)
The author with Mike during TT practice, 1978
Mike catches Read in Ramsey in the 1978 F1 TT (*Cecil Bailey*)
The 1978 F1 TT – Hailwood about to pass Read (*John Everett*)
Mick Grant on his way to winning the 1978 Classic TT (*Adrian Ashurst*)
Practising on the 1979 Ducati (*Daily Mirror*)
The 1979 Senior – Mike on the 500 Suzuki (*Daily Mirror*)
Mike, Ted Macauley, and 'Cat's Eyes' Cunningham (*Leslie Bryce*)
The wreckage of Mike's Rover after the fatal accident
Pauline Hailwood arrives for the funeral (*Daily Mirror*)
Mike's coffin is borne from the church (*Daily Mirror*)
A winner – on the Honda 250-6...
And on the 1978 900cc Ducati... (*C. Edwards and Son*)
And after the 1978 F1 TT (*Adrian Ashurst*)

To live on in hearts we leave behind is
not to leave at all ...

1

Death of a Legend

The sharp rasp of a motor-bike being stressed through its gears crackled across the silence which 3,000 people shared on a peaceful hillside at Braddan Bridge, alongside the TT course on the Isle of Man.

It was a gentle summer's day ... one morning in June 1981. The slight breeze hardly rustled the highest leaves in the trees or stirred the long grass on the slopes behind old Braddan church, but it carried the sound of the motor-bike into that idyllic patch until its echoes faded and died in the distance. It was an eerie reminder, as if we needed one, of Mike, the man whom we all loved, and whose memory we were honouring at an outdoor memorial service on the island where, over the years, so many had come to worship his achievements.

That anonymous rider could not have known how dramatically he underlined the feeling of loss we were all privately suffering; neither could the timing have been more appropriate. For I had struggled against quickly filling eyes and a choking throat to say from the pulpit: 'To live on in hearts we leave behind is not to die at all ...' My eyes ranged across a congregation of absolute sadness to where Mike's widow Pauline and his sister Chris were cuddling each other

Mike

in a mutual search for warmth and comfort, trying to overcome the hurt and cruelty of a tragedy that had claimed not only the great man's life but his daughter Michelle's too.

Behind them stood ranks of good friends. And all around, as far as the eye could see to the farthest heights of the hillside, were people who knew Mike only as a face on television or in the newspapers or magazines but who respected his genius and loved him for his modesty. All joined in one tearful goodbye on a morning none of them would forget.

When it was all over and done with, when the traffic in the narrow lane alongside the church had unjammed itself and the rickety pulpit from which I had read the lesson stood in quiet isolation and the priestly resonance had faded, there was left only an emptiness of feeling amongst a huge audience as it departed, travelling across a stage which had lost its greatest performer.

The TT course, nearly thirty-eight miles of the most challenging stretch of racing in the history of the sport, swerves under the shadow of Braddan church's high tower. Only two years before, many of those at the memorial service had packed the makeshift grandstand overlooking the treacherously adverse-cambered bridge at Braddan and marvelled at the magnificence of Mike in full flow, chased by a pack of youngsters on thoroughbred racing machinery, howling after his reputation.

Who, in their wildest nightmare, could have ever believed that Mike was destined to die in such ironic circumstances? What wicked twist of fate determined that the greatest motor-cycle racer of all time should survive a career spent on the very threshold of disaster – on the world's most dangerous circuits at the highest possible speeds and with the greatest risks undertaken – only to be killed in a road crash that was no fault of his own?

His death would have been far more acceptable had it happened in the hurly-burly of fierce competition; but then in all the years I had known him, across all the countries and circuits I had seen him race, he had never seemed to me to be in the remotest danger of coming to any great grief when the

Death of a Legend

issue was in his own hands. Such was his skill. It was based on a firm bedrock of daring, but with coldly calculated moves only attempted when the sureness of the outcome was virtually guaranteed; he could not, of course, legislate for the errors of others which might sweep him up, or the occasionally inevitable failure of machinery which might pitch him off.

I cannot recall, in the twenty-one years I watched him compete at the highest level for the sport's richest rewards, any moments of genuine complaint from rivals about his attitude, or any accusations of ruthlessness or unfair tactics. He raced to win. And that meant he raced hard. But he asked no favours, granted none, and accepted that a will to win often took a man into areas from which he would normally shy away, but which had to be inhabited in order to stir the best from one's reserve of skills. He told me he only once cheated, but that it was more in fun than with any evil intent to deprive an opponent of victory.

He chose as his dupe – though it was not premeditated – the rather dour, straight-faced Derek Minter, a big star of the 1950s and 1960s, and a brilliant rider who was almost unbeatable at Brands Hatch, the circuit he considered home ground. They were neck and neck, precocious young ace Hailwood and the veteran Minter, heading towards the final bend at Brands after a tremendous tussle that had forced the vast crowd to its feet.

'I knew I couldn't beat him fair and square,' Mike told me years later. 'I was squeezing everything I could out of my bike and it wouldn't go a yard quicker. But we were side by side and I looked across at him. He just stared back, those big eyes of his popping behind his goggles looking daggers at me. He started to smile ... you know ... that confident smile you get when you know you're going to win. And I wasn't going to have that and on a sheer reflex I suddenly jerked my head up, glanced towards his back wheel and pointed frantically down towards it. It must have scared the wits out of him. I'll bet he thought it was about to fall off, because he suddenly sat up and when he did it was enough to leave me clear and I shot away to win.

Mike

'Jesus, he was mad. He realised right away what had happened, but it was too late for him to do anything about it. I thought he was going to kill me. But I was bloody remorseful about it. I hated myself for ages – but later I saw the funny side of it and I couldn't help laughing every time Mint's face came into my mind. Minter of all people! And at Brands! It's a wonder he didn't take a contract out on me. But I never did that sort of thing to anybody ever again. It was my big lesson.'

Hailwood was something of an old-fashioned Corinthian in many ways; the sporting attitude was pure even if the instinct and the hunger for victory were intense. That way all his race rivals knew exactly what to expect when the flag dropped; wherever they were at the finish, first or last, if they had given him a good chase, if only for a moment or two, in any confrontation he always made sure he told them he had enjoyed it or appreciated their ability to force him into stronger action. And there were very many no-hopers over the years who were given this particularly welcome sort of blessing and to whom it became the highpoint of an otherwise undistinguished career.

None of this is being wise with hindsight, or trying to give greater legend to the man than already existed. It is merely an attempt to spread to a wider audience the rather privileged view I had of him at close quarters. I suppose his death has brought into sharper focus some of the folklore that grew up around him, a lot of it hardly noticed by him, and much of it seemingly unimportant until now, when it seems to me to be hugely vital for an understanding of Mike's make-up, and of the universal appeal and adoration he commanded without necessarily enjoying or even, at times, understanding it.

He was frequently genuinely puzzled and, therefore, greatly embarrassed by the unashamed affection people showed him. His shrinking back from it was often mistaken for an uncaring conceit and an arrogance which people could be quite scathing about. That hurt him too. So we had this bundle of contradictions tied up inside one man: on the one hand he hated all the fuss, and on the other he disliked

Death of a Legend

having to fight against all his natural instincts and accept it with a ready smile and a reluctantly returned handshake. It was a credit to his awareness that he did make some attempt, however forced, to accept happily that which most embarrassed him – even if his response to the adulation was a watered-down one.

That embarrassment would have been total if he could have seen the turn-out both at the memorial service on the Isle of Man and at his funeral at his country home near Birmingham. For it was as great a demonstration of affection for the man as he would ever have wished to avoid.

The police were so concerned that the winding country lanes of Warwickshire's stockbroker-belt would be so violated by the sound of motor-bikes heading for the funeral in Mike's village church that they wanted to ban bikes from the area and set up stop-points to filter them out. They believed they were acting in good faith, I suppose, but their assumptions were all awry. These, after all, were the people who felt close to Mike, who had been enraptured by his talent and devastated by his death, and who wanted quite properly to pay their last respects. And Pauline, despite her grief at losing not only a husband but a lovely little daughter too, and in spite of massive doses of tranquillisers, realised that these bikers had as much right to feel they should be there as those closest friends who had travelled from the other side of the world.

And quite rightly so. There is a unique camaraderie among motor-cyclists. Mike had been part of it, and a brilliant exponent of the sport which was at its heart; and he was revered, of course, as the man who had given motor-cycling its firmest credibility and respectability. To deny bikers the chance to attend would have been unforgivable; the police came to realise it and local doubts were quickly dissolved. In the event the bikers made it a memorable and moving occasion – they stood in freezing rain on a most inhospitable morning, tears scarcely distinguishable from the rain on their cheeks, content to be in the street if they could not squeeze into the crowded church. Long hair tumbling over unshaven faces. Leather

Mike

jackets. Studs. Heavy belts. Garish helmets. Tough characters. Boys and girls. Older bikers with goggles and aged skid-lids and even older machines. Side-cars. Mopeds. Any form of transport that would get them there; and they, again, travelled from all over the country. They mingled and wept with James Hunt and Giacomo Agostini and Derek Bell and David Hobbs. With John Surtees and a desperately grieving Luigi Taveri, the little Swiss who had been in the Honda team with Mike, and who could not understand all that was going on because he spoke so little English. Michelle's tiny white coffin was set side by side in front of the altar with Mike's, as close together as they had been the night their lives ended.

Looking back, even after three years, I still feel the chill of the church, the unremitting sadness and sense of loss, the enduring memory of Pauline's helplessness, and the desperate unreality of it all. As if it was all happening to somebody else and I was merely an onlooker rather than at the centre of it all.

In a lifetime of racing I had been too often too close to friends who had died. I had suffered greatly but had always got over it, working on the premise that they were men who fully understood the risks, were ready to accept them, and who knew that fate could only decree that some of them in such a dangerous pursuit must die. I had almost – not entirely – become inured to the cold fact that from time to time I would lose good friends in numbers far greater than those lost to people outside the sport of racing. But I could not, and still cannot, accept or understand that Mike should be killed in the way he was; it was the strangest twist of fate there could be. A road accident had managed to do what hundreds of thousands of racing miles had never even come close to achieving; the red, white and gold helmet, fixed to the lid of Mike's coffin, did not have even a scratch on it.

Only ten days before I followed in the procession from the church of St Mary Magdalene at Tanworth-in-Arden, a couple of miles from what had been Mike's happy home, I had been startled from deep sleep by the phone ringing at 6.30 a.m. And you know, you just know, that it cannot

Death of a Legend

possibly be anything but bad news when the phone rings at that time in the morning.

'Prepare yourself for a shock. Mike's been in a big crash ... he's badly hurt ... and I don't think he'll live. Little Michelle's been killed. But Davy's okay. Just a bump on the head. Nothing else.'

It was the tired and weary voice of Rod Sawyer, a long-time friend of Mike's from his early car-racing days, calling from an office in the Birmingham accident unit. The administration director had set him up with a phone and a desk and Rod was busy telephoning Mike's nearest friends with the dread news.

Only yards away Mike was on a breathing machine in the intensive care unit. Pauline was with him. But he was so badly and irreversibly injured that there was barely any life. Not even hope. Not a flicker in a world that had turned dark for him. He was deeply unconscious, unaware of anything that had happened, unable even to drum up fight in that enormous chest of his. Only the ventilator maintained his tenuous link with a life that was drawing to its close. Pauline's sedation was some defence against the horror of it all.

Mike's brain stem had been severed. His throat cut. His jaw was shattered, his right arm broken, his left leg and ankle too, and he had internal injuries on a massive scale. He had taken the full impact of the crash and it was only a matter of time before that great heart gave out. Even if he had lived, he would have been a helpless cripple, a vegetable – at least there was in death some dignity reserved for him.

He hung on for two days, but on Monday 23 March 1981 he died. The challenge had been too grave even for a fighter like him.

'I was with him when he died,' said Sawyer. 'He was in a deep coma. The dot on the support machine suddenly started to go haywire and a nurse said very gently "It won't be long now" – and within ten minutes or so he had gone. That lovely man had gone ... it was unbelievable because you knew that if he had been able to have a say in it, he would have fought and battled back.'

Mike

Fears that the hospital had turned off the ventilating machine because of the hopelessness of Mike's case were dismissed by Peter Millward, the administrator.

'Nothing like that happened,' he said. 'Mike was still on the life-support when he passed away. His injuries were so severe he never really had a chance of survival. We looked after him in our Major Injuries Unit and he could not have had better care, nor could he have been admitted much quicker. The Unit is right up against the entrance where the ambulances draw up and within seconds of his arrival he was on the ventilator. We specialise in the treatment of trauma and Mike was in good hands from the moment he arrived, but it was a hopeless situation.'

Pauline, heavily sedated, was given a room close to the five-bed unit where Mike was located. 'But I don't think ... mercifully ... she realised quite what was going on,' said Sawyer. 'The hospital had eased that pain for her as much as they could.'

Sawyer was without sleep for thirty-six hours. 'I just lived on coffee and brandy,' he said. 'There were so many calls to make and answer right around the world.'

He had been at his home near London when a neighbour of Mike's phoned him to give the news of the crash. 'The police were marvellous,' said Sawyer. 'They cleared the way for me to Birmingham. But when I got to the hospital, the report was disastrous. There was no chance at all for Mike, and Michelle was dead. Davy was virtually unscathed, just a bump on his head, but miraculously he had survived this most horrendous crash otherwise unhurt.

'I never set foot outside the admin office. It seemed that everybody in the world wanted to call and they were all willing Mike to live. And the sad thing was they all said the same thing: if it was within Mike's control, he would survive okay. But it was right out of his hands. I knew what the outcome was going to be, even though I couldn't tell people outside.

'I was at Mike's bedside as often as I could be, and he was awfully knocked about. He had been cleaned up as best the hospital could, but he was in a sad state.

Death of a Legend

'When the inevitable happened and my job at the hospital was finished, I was amazed that I had been awake so long ... just about two days without so much as a wink of sleep. In between times I must have talked to a thousand people on the phone.'

Sawyer's cool, organisational expertise eased Pauline's burden over the following months; he set up a sort of committee of close friends to try and unravel Mike's complicated finances, to work out the funeral arrangements, to take as much heartbreak as possible out of Pauline's life and generally, with his wife Jenny, to be the buffer between her and the problems she was about to face as she was let down from the sedation that had kept her sane.

It says much for Pauline's strength of character that she was able to struggle through the darkest days of her life and emerge as she is now, three years later, a well-balanced woman of some achievement, able, despite her despair, to bring up her son David without suffocating him with too intense a love – which would be very easy to do after such a traumatic episode. Her memories of Mike and Michelle sustain her and boost her during the moments when her thoughts naturally wander back to the evening of the crash – the last time she saw them alive.

There is nothing particularly hazardous about the A435 dual carriageway that winds south out of Birmingham and cuts through the pleasant countryside into deep Warwickshire – but, like all roads, circumstances dramatically alter cases. And Saturday 21 March 1981 was a particularly filthy night; grey drizzle, spray, fudged horizons and a twilight so tricky that it all added up to a severe test of eyesight, even for Mike. And there is no doubt that he had the sharpest all-seeing eyes and the quickest reflexes of anybody I have known. They had seen him safely through enough crises on the circuits to underline that fact. Road-driving with him was never a terrifying journey for passengers sitting alongside. He was smooth, unhurried, never flustered by the idiocy that often threatens from other, less caring drivers, and certainly he never took his Grand Prix dash onto the open road, more especially if he was with his two children

Mike

and his wife. He was a model of calmness.

Mike had sold his big Mercedes and was using a Rover the night he arrived home from his motor-cycle sales business in Birmingham. He and his partner, Rod Gould, the former world 250cc champion, were not happy with the way the recession had devastated the Midlands and had hit their company – and they were struggling to keep it afloat. So, obviously, Mike had plenty to think about, a lot on his mind. This was plain from the way his usual happy-go-lucky style of life had somewhat slowed up and been changed by the day-to-day worries of business and the huge capital investment he had made, the guarantees he had undertaken and his ambitions to make a go of it.

How much all this could have impaired his concentration is impossible to assess, but his friend Rod Sawyer felt it might have contributed something to the events that followed. His view was firmly based, for he had been close to Mike throughout this worrying time. He, like me, had seen Mike in more despair because of the business than at any other time in his life. And even on the evening of the crash Mike had spent about one and a half hours on the phone to Sawyer, pouring his heart out about his disappointments and worries. I'd had a similar experience, with Mike so unusually serious, so uncharacteristically gloomy, on a long flight back from Miami to London only two weeks previously. But almost as quickly as the mood had brought him low, he lifted himself up again and was his usual mischievous self, glowing with the fun that was more typical of him.

Sawyer recalls: 'Mike was feeling pretty miserable that night. Business was bad, and he was dreadfully low about it. We chatted for ages on the phone and he said he could see no future in it. The shop had been burgled again as well and the video stolen once more, and it all added up to Mike's general depression. He couldn't understand the pettiness of the thieves ... he couldn't get over the way the recession had hit the company, and he wasn't happy doing what he was doing.

'I mean, he was loading and unloading bikes. Making

Death of a Legend

deliveries in the van. Selling and being a front man in the showroom – and, quite frankly, it just was not his scene. But, with his usual enthusiasm and honesty, he felt that if it would benefit the business he should do it. Another man, so deeply committed financially, might have been happy to stay a sleeping partner and sit back and enjoy his fame and his reputation without putting in any effort. Not Mike. He couldn't be like that ... but it all served to undermine him as the character of old. And this was the situation and the mood he was in the night he crashed.'

Whatever depressive background there was, I feel sure that Mike's concentration would have been as keen as ever as he moved easily along the A435 bringing Davy and Michelle back from a fish-and-chips supper treat just a few miles away. Michelle, as she usually did, was sitting in the front passenger seat. Davy, in the back, cuddled his fluffy toy cat. He was probably in his regular place, standing between the front seats looking ahead through the windscreen.

For a man who had lived so close to the edge all his racing life there was nothing, *under normal circumstances*, that could have imperilled or threatened Mike's control that night; conditions were well within his reactions and his capability, even though they might have been a test for an ordinary road user. There was an attempt to suggest that Mike, being a racing driver, would have been speeding excessively, but this was a slur that was quickly disproved, not only by a couple who were following him, but by a splendid piece of police work that removed all lingering doubts about whether any blame at all could be attributed to Mike.

When he was suddenly confronted with the direst of difficulties, not even Mike's flash reactions could steer him clear. A flat-bed truck that had been running ahead of him swung in a loop over to the left of the carriageway, then pulled to the right to make an illegal U-turn through a coned-off emergency cut-through to the adjoining, opposite-running carriageway. Yet only 150 yards or so further on there was a slip road off the main road; the truck

Mike

could have used this to cross quite legally to the other carriageway and complete its journey without causing any danger. As it was, in the minute or so which the driver was attempting to save, the finest motor-cycle racer the world had ever seen was killed, along with his daughter. Mike was a few days short of his forty-first birthday. Michelle was nine.

The lorry driver, Raymond Whitmore, a 50-year-old from Kingswinford in neighbouring West Midlands, was fined £100 with £105 costs for careless driving. He later made an appeal against the conviction at Warwick Crown Court, but it was dismissed.

The owner of the truck, Eric Darby, from Hollywood, Worcestershire, was fined £160 with £30 costs after admitting that the vehicle had no insurance – and that Whitmore had been allowed to drive it even though he had no licence to do so. His solicitor, Mr John McMillan, told the magistrates at Stratford-upon-Avon that Darby faced ruin if the Hailwood estate claimed against him.

Mike's family had been devastated and the events surrounding the incident had left their mark on the minds not only of those close to the Hailwoods but people on the periphery too. People like Mr and Mrs Ronald Pharo, a Birmingham chemist and his wife, a former nurse, who were following Mike's car in their own and who were lucky not to be caught up in the devastation.

Mr Pharo recalled: 'It was an absolutely awful night … drizzly, but not foggy. But sort of misty and very dark, really miserable. I can't remember any car at all overtaking me, so Mike must have been ahead of me all the time; there was certainly no substance to any suggestion that he had gone belting by me. Definitely not. I would have noticed anybody overtaking me. It was important to be concentrating on what was happening and I could not have failed to notice had another car gone past at any speed, slow or fast. So there was no question at all of him racing through.

'You know, the age-old nonsense that he *must* have been speeding simply because he was a racing driver can set up all sorts of misconceptions. My view was not coloured either

Death of a Legend

one way or the other – I had no idea at all who was involved in the crash until I read it in the newspapers and heard about it on the radio the day afterwards. It seems to me that whatever assumptions were made about Mike speeding were only arrived at *after* it was known who he was, and that was totally unfair.

'We must have been about 300 yards behind Mike's Rover ... there was another car, a Porsche, in between us ... and I suppose we came onto the scene of the crash about thirty seconds after it had happened. I'll never forget it ... it was so distressing ... the most awful and sad thing I had ever experienced in my life.

'The man in the Porsche, quite a young fellow, was very lucky indeed. He had been that much closer when the lorry swung out to the left then turned back to the right to cut through the opening in the central reservation to go down the opposite side of the carriageway. He had seen it all at close quarters, and yet somehow managed to steer his car through the debris and the bedlam. When I pulled up, the Porsche was already stopped and the young man was being sick. He couldn't do anything to help he was so distressed, and he kept on apologising for being so stunned into helplessness.

'The Rover was a wreck, barely recognisable. The roof was torn back. The horn was blaring, there was smoke pouring out of the engine and the smell of petrol in the air was overpowering. It was difficult in the dark and because of the mess, but I found the battery leads and disconnected them to stop the noise of the horn and reduce the risk of fire. Right away I could see the fellow behind the wheel was in a really bad way – his head looked quite badly injured. I just wanted to make sure he wasn't being choked by blood or anything, so I made attempts to keep his air passages clear.

'He was still alive and breathing, but he was deeply unconscious and trapped. There was no way I could get him out and I decided to leave that until the rescue services arrived. The lorry driver or somebody with him had gone to phone for help.

'The little girl alongside Mike seemed to be trapped as well

Mike

– by the legs – and Mary, my wife, went to do what she could. There was not a mark on her face – she seemed to have taken the impact on her chest. Mary said she was breathing, but she, too, was knocked out ... mercifully because obviously she was badly hurt. She died about four minutes later as my wife held her hand. It was heartbreaking. But it was evident that Mike never knew what had happened and certainly never realised that his little girl had been killed.

'There was another passer-by briefly on the scene. A woman who said she was a nurse who had two children with her. She told us there was nothing that anybody could do for Mike or Michelle, and she was right. We just felt we had to stay with them. Then, to our utter amazement, we found a little boy in the wreckage, down in the footwell at the back. He started howling like mad, and when we got him out, we saw he had survived with only a bump on his head.

'Considering the rural situation, the ambulance and the police were there in no time at all, maybe ten minutes at the most. But there was no way either Mike or his daughter could have been saved. To all intents and purposes they were dead at the scene. I know Mike lived on a couple of days longer, but really he had died alongside Michelle that night.

'It was quite incredible that young David escaped; it was the one spark of happiness and joy my wife and I had in a terrible scene. The upset which we both suffered was enough to stay with us for the rest of our lives, and not being able to do anything other than comfort as best we could is a bitter memory – but they were beyond any help.

'It's a particularly bad stretch of road where the crash happened. I call it the Bermuda Triangle, there have been so many crashes there. I had a bad one myself nearby – another car ran into the back of mine and my wife was injured.

'I think Mike was left without a prayer of a chance when the truck pulled across him. If it could catch out a man of his reflexes, what chance for anybody else? I managed to avoid the debris without any difficulty, but the man in the Porsche had one hell of a scare. He was in a terrible state at the scene, throwing up and in shock, and I can understand why. He

Death of a Legend

has all my sympathy and I have no criticism at all to offer. He had not only seen it all, he just missed getting caught up in it. No wonder he couldn't bring himself to do anything. He could quite easily have been one of the victims.'

The lorry driver, perhaps because he was too shocked, stood by his vehicle throughout Mr Pharo's rescue effort and his wife's bid to comfort Michelle. He chatted, apparently unemotionally, to people at the scene but never went across either to assist or check what was happening. Soon after the crash, he underwent an eye-correction operation to cure a long-standing fault.

Police Constable Mike Anslow, who was stationed in the village and who knew Mike, Pauline and the children, was on general patrol in his Panda car when he picked up the emergency call from Control to go to the scene at nearby Portway.

'Michelle had been thrown against the dashboard and she was already dead when I got there. Mike was trapped in the driving seat ... he was lying back, but his legs were stuck. There were signs of life: his breathing was very gurgly but he was alive. However, I could see he was quite badly injured. The fire brigade got to work very quickly and pulled him and Michelle clear.

'I hadn't realised who it was, though I thought I recognised the car number when it was being passed to Swansea records for a check-up. When I arrived at the scene, I knew right away, of course, that it was Mike.

'I had been up to the house quite a few times. The burglar alarm was always going off and I had got to know the family quite well – they always made me a cup of tea and chatted. Ever so friendly. So it was all doubly upsetting for me. Crashes are bad enough as it is, but when kids are involved and get hurt and killed it knocks you back.'

He surveyed the chaos, the rubble and debris, with Mike's car slewed over to the left, and saw that only a little way up the road was the slipway up which the lorry driver could have gone before turning, safely, to go back in the direction from which he had come. 'Instead', Anslow said, 'he decided to take the short-cut through the intersection. That was fatal.'

Mike

Constable John O'Dell was on patrol on the evening shift, some distance from Portway, when he had a radio message to hurry to the A435 to attend a crash.

'I was the second car there. Mike Anslow had already arrived ... and the whole scene was a mess. Quite horrific – as bad as anything I had ever seen in all my years on traffic duty.

'Mike's car was on the left-hand side of the carriageway in a severe state of damage. The roof had been torn right back, though there was very little damage below windscreen height. The top had been folded back to the nearside corner. Mike, by then, had been taken to the Birmingham accident hospital and Michelle to the mortuary.

'I did what I could at the scene and was then ordered to collect Mrs Hailwood and take her to the hospital. We had to drive past the accident on the other carriageway, but I don't think she had any idea. She was too concerned to get to hospital and too shocked to realise fully what had happened.'

In fact, Constable O'Dell's interest did not end there; he was not happy that there might be suggestions that Mike had been speeding or had been in some way at fault. But his instincts told him Mike was blameless and, even though it might have embarrassed his senior officers more than a little, he set about painstakingly removing any shadow of doubt from the issue. He undertook a brilliant piece of jigsaw work that was a credit to his dedication and which reflected brightly on police thoroughness.

All the experience which he had gained in ten years he put into showing that wherever the blame lay, it most certainly was not with Mike – and even though he faced quite a fight in court, his reconstruction, so cleverly thought out, was totally accepted as being an accurate picture of what had happened. The defence collapsed in the face of it.

When he arrived at the scene of the accident that night, the truck had already been removed, so all his work had to be done later. He and a breakdown expert took over a yard, manhandling the wreckage of Mike's Rover and inching their way over the truck until the damaged pieces slotted

Death of a Legend

together into a telling pattern of evidence which revealed the angle of impact and demonstrated irrefutably that the lorry driver had blundered disastrously.

Constable O'Dell's tireless and revealing efforts cleared Mike's name and it was a source of great relief to this conscientious officer that they proved so worthwhile.

'I like to see that things are right,' he said, 'and I felt that something was very wrong with the way it was going and what was being said. That's why I persisted in my investigations.'

He knew that Mike had been faced suddenly with a side-on view of the flat-bed of an eight-ton truck whose lights would be barely, if at all, visible at the rear. After that, as Mike tried to make a last split-second turn, the Rover hit the unloaded flat-bed, which, only a matter of inches deep, sliced into the car at chest height, smashing down the screen and its supports, tearing back the roof like a can opener, hitting Mike fatally across the top half of his body and sending Michelle plunging against the dashboard.

'It would all have happened so quickly,' said the Constable, 'that Mike would have been unconscious almost before he had realised his predicament. He would have been totally powerless to do anything.'

It was Constable Mike Anslow's job to supervise the indentification formalities after Mike had died. The pathologist told him: 'Mike's was one of the fittest bodies I have ever seen, particularly in a man of his age.' But not even that attribute could get Mike through this last great crisis of his life.

David, who was seven, had some glass removed from his chin and was allowed to go home. He watched pictures of the pile-up on television and saw his cuddly cat in the wreckage ... and broke down. Rod Sawyer, who had collected him from hospital, had to go and retrieve Davy's favourite toy.

The inquests on Mike and Michelle were held in front of Dr John Brown, the Warwickshire coroner, in July 1981, four months after the crash, and he recorded verdicts of accidental death. Officially, he found, they had both died from head injuries.

Mike

The driver of the lorry, Raymond Whitmore, refused to give evidence at the hearing, but in a statement given earlier to the police he had said he was travelling in a straight line when the collision happened. He felt a bump and his lorry was pushed across the central reservation of the dual carriageway. He said he could remember nothing more about the accident.

PC John O'Dell's evidence refuted the driver's assertions and he told the inquest that he had reconstructed the incident and his experiments showed that the lorry had turned through between sixty and seventy degrees before the impact. Coroner Dr Brown said there was a direct conflict of evidence and added that O'Dell's contribution was of great value.

Three months afterwards, a three-hour hearing at Stratford-upon-Avon magistrates' court found 50-year-old Whitmore, a driver of some thirty-five years' experience, guilty of careless driving. He said he stood by the statement he had made to the police in which, he claimed, he had made no move towards the gaps in the carriageway to complete a U-turn. His lawyer, Giles Peppercorn, asked the magistrates to consider that the real culprit that night had been the appalling weather conditions. In March 1982, a year after Mike's and Michelle's deaths, the driver lost his appeal against the conviction.

It was a year of readjustment for Pauline, a testing time in which she had to battle through a legacy of awesome problems and difficulties, even a fall-out with unthinking neighbours. Finally, she moved away from the area to a beautiful home, much smaller, further south – but still not clear of the memories that haunted her. And still there were more legal issues to be settled, more battles to be fought.

2

Pauline's Story, and More ...

In the summer of 1981, only months after the fatal accident, Pauline was invited to go to the Isle of Man – a move supported by the Manx tourist authorities and the TT Supporters' Club, of which Mike had been President – to attend the races that Mike had almost made his own personal property. It was a galling situation for her, but one from which she could not escape. The reminders were everywhere; the memories of Mike's island achievements were non-stop, and, of course, well-wishers meaning to be kind seemed to be around every corner.

I thought Pauline was extremely brave. She accepted the invitation without really knowing what was going to happen or even how to deal with it, and she was taken from ceremony to ceremony without particularly wanting to be so deeply involved. It was, after all, Mike's world really, and while she had been part of it, she did not fully understand that much about it when it came to TT matters, personalities and places to be. It was an emotionally charged trip and I am not sure she should have accepted the invitation. I am not sure either that there was not some cashing-in, in the sense that Mike's name was being exploited through Pauline. But it certainly came home to me that she should *not* have

Mike

undertaken the trip when I bumped into her at the reception desk of the Palace in Douglas, the island's most prestigious hotel. She was settling her own bill. I was astonished, to say the least. Pauline was signing a cheque, and this was a time when money was not readily available to her; Mike's financial situation had hardly been sorted out and there was Pauline, far too nice to complain, paying the bill for a trip she was reluctant to make and which had been exploited both by the Manx authorities and the TT Supporters' Club. To say I was angry is to put it mildly – but Pauline, bless her, did not want to make any fuss, so I kept quiet about it.

It reminded me of a situation that Mike had got himself into when he agreed to make a film for a man who didn't even bother to take out the necessary insurance on Mike's life or limbs, even though Mike was doing the chap a favour by riding a bike with a camera attachment. We did not find out until it was too late that the premium – about £125 and the least the man could do in return for the favour – had not been paid. Mike, like Pauline, did not want to cause any ill-feeling, though he was desperately angry and felt cheated. As I stood there in the Palace Hotel, I suddenly realised how similar in attitude they both were. Each spent a lifetime in the main trusting that the people around them would neither short-change them nor do anything to betray the warm friendship which they each offered so freely. Yet whoever it was who was responsible for arranging Pauline's Isle of Man trip showed scant regard for her. And when you think the bill was in total something like £200, pin money to an authority, or to a club, the pettiness of it all is staggering.

At the 1982 TT, one year after Mike's death, there had been a lot of pomp and ceremony and talk about what memorials to the great man could be set up or stationed around the course. A bench beside the circuit, a statue, a grandstand, a plaque – these were just some of the ideas floated. Then I discovered, to my bitter amazement, that the authorities at the centre of all this memorial talk had forgotten even to include in the official programme for the race – all 22,500 copies of it – two stretches of the course which had been named after him and which should have

Pauline's Story, and More ...

been shown on the centre-page plan: Hailwood Rise and Hailwood Heights. But I could find no reference anywhere, only one year after the greatest TT rider of them all had been killed, on any of the maps issued by the Auto-Cycle Union, organisers of the race.

It was an oversight, as careless as the one that had caused Pauline's concern at the hotel. Nor was I the only person upset by it. A friend of Mike's, Bob Grimshaw, who ran the Hailwood Bar in the Crosby Hotel at the Highlander section of the TT course, a few miles beyond the start-and-finish line, was furious.

Bob's bar was like a shrine to Mike, and any disregard for his memory was considered by him as a massive insult. The two of them had become firm friends when Mike made his fairy-tale comeback to the TT in 1978. Every time he broke down in practice, he always seemed to end up in the bar at the Crosby Hotel, Bob's pub, waiting to be picked up. Mike's total lack of pretension confirmed Bob's unashamed admiration for his island exploits, and Bob persuaded the brewery which controlled his business to help him develop the Hailwood Bar with its endless photographs and souvenirs.

Bob's rage was intense: 'How quickly people forget,' he said. 'It's a scandal, a disgrace, that Mike's name should be left off the map. That programme goes to every part of the racing world – and it goes without the memory of the man who brought it so much honour.' The Auto-Cycle Union's embarrassment was deep: Secretary Ken Shierson apologised for the oversight and promised to correct it the following year, which he did.

At the same time donations were flooding in for some sort of memorial on the island. The 180-bed Birmingham Accident Unit, too, was being deluged and administrator Peter Millward said: 'In no time at all we had about £20,000 which was used to buy vital medical equipment. It was fantastic, really, that people from all over the world wanted to associate themselves with the fund, and their financial support in Mike's name went a long way towards improving the life-saving efforts of the hospital. Mike would certainly

Mike

have been proud of the response.'

For a long time afterwards Pauline kept in touch with the hospital. The policeman, Mike Anslow, kept his eye on the house in its idyllically secluded patch behind some trees on the main road that skirted the village that Mike had made his home. Anslow, in fact, used to call in with little toys for David; he would do anything he could do to keep the boy's mind off those traumatic, nightmarish moments. And he was a great source of practical help.

Pauline was surrounded by gentle, caring friends. For the hurt felt by a woman who had lost not only a husband but a daughter too, needed a special brand of courage from her and a good deal of support from those close to her.

I can recall journeying from my home in Manchester to see her and take her to a film show all about Mike at a police club in Birmingham. The funds were to go to the hospital and Pauline felt she should attend even though she fully understood it was likely to be a gruelling experience for her. Barely six months had passed since the crash, and when Mike's smiling face spread across the giant screen, it was the first time since he had been killed that Pauline had seen him walking, talking and moving. It was a profoundly moving experience. Pauline gripped my hand and bit her bottom lip in a stupendous effort not to cry out. How she did not break down I will never know. Mike had put all his bravery on show when he won his George Medal; now, I felt, it was Pauline's turn to be brave. All she had to win, though, was a peace of mind that was all too elusive when there were so many reminders that kept bringing Mike to life in her mind's eye. The sadness showed in those bright blue eyes of hers, and there were times, even six months later, when she still seemed stunned by the despair and helplessness of it all.

We sat in her comfy lounge and the memories of Mike were everywhere – pictures, trophies, winner's sashes, medals, world championship certificates and paintings. She stared out of the lattice windows into the long garden where Mike used to romp with the kids and said:

'When we were at the film show and I saw him up there on the screen, it took all the control I could muster not to burst

Pauline's Story, and More ...

out crying. It was a weird feeling suddenly to see him, but I know it's something I'll have to train myself to get used to because there are so many films and pictures of him around that I suppose they'll keep on cropping up every now and again. But looking at him then, so fit and healthy, it was as if I had suddenly woken up from a nightmare and he and Michelle were still alive. And I had bad-dreamed it all.

'It's odd, you know, with all these reminders of him.' She swept an arm around the walls of the lounge. 'You might think it would be upsetting. But it's not. They keep him fresh in my mind. They go a long way to keeping me sane. Every one of them bears some special little memory for me. And I have changed nothing. I have kept the house just as it was the night he and Michelle went out and never came back.

'I find it difficult to understand those people who throw everything away – the clothes, the precious pictures – and try to wipe out the pain of what really is a precious memory of somebody they loved with all their heart. I keep on telling myself that it's as if he has gone racing and will be away for a while, just like he always was. That way I don't expect him to walk in through the door any second ... and that way I hope I'll be able to persuade myself that neither he nor Michelle are coming home to me ever again.'

She held on to Davy so tightly that I thought she'd crush all the air out of him. The little boy with Mike's determination – enough to win a ski-ing bronze medal his first time on the slopes – is a double of his father at the same age. Like Mike the kid, he too rides a mini-bike with flair and lawn-ripping dash.

Pauline, talking as she had not done since the crash, was happy and relieved to open up a little and give vent to all the terrible frustration and bitterness which had inevitably built up. Little Davy still had nightmares six months afterwards.

'He never talks about it when he's awake, though he must have some terrible memories of that night. He keeps it all locked up – but I do hear him jabbering away when he's asleep, so his mind is obviously still in a turmoil. Strangely, he missed Michelle far more than he missed Mike. I suppose

Mike

it was because Mike was away so often and Michelle was his best pal and playmate as well as his sister. They were really good chums. All he said to me, later, was "Mummy, I'll be able to sleep in your bed now that Daddy's not coming back." It was heartbreaking, but to him it was the most important thing in his life; he just wanted to be close, I guess, didn't want to feel left out and to get in my bed was his answer.

'I don't know what must have been going on in his mind because a little time later he absolutely staggered me by asking me why I didn't get married again. And when I asked him why, he said he wanted a daddy. I had to explain as best I could that I still loved Mike very much and that I couldn't possibly love anybody else, so he'd just have to make do with me. But I could see he was being terribly brave.

'To have lost two beings you loved so much is unbearable. I had no idea just how much of my life and thoughts they occupied until they were not there any longer. Mike was such a lovely man. I used to look at him when he didn't know I was doing it and think that he could not be the same guy who had done all those incredibly brave things. He was like two men, really. One at home, loving and just a family man proud of his kids, happy to be with me, and serenely content with a circle of smashing mates. The other, a devil-may-care hero, a swashbuckling idol to millions, loved by people all over the world, the typically dashing Englishman everybody loves to love. It's the *hero* everybody knows. But to me he was just my *husband*. Just a nice guy to live with.

'He was such a fine man, strong and resilient, the ideal type to have children by; with nothing showing on the surface that would ever make you believe he was the same man who had done all those wonderful things and achieved all that he had.

'You know, I have never told anybody before,' she confided, 'but a few years ago I went to see a palmist. Mike would have taken the mickey and scoffed at the whole idea, but I went secretly and kept quite about it. She told me that in 1974 I would have a great moment of joy – and one of

Pauline's Story, and More ...

sadness. And she was so right: David was born in May, then in August Mike had that terrible crash in a racing-car at the West German Grand Prix at the Nürburgring. His worst ever. It left him with a limp that he had until the day he died, and it bloody near killed him at the time.

'Then I remembered later that she told me that the man I loved would go out of my life in his thirty-sixth or thirty-seventh year. So when Mike went back to the Isle of Man for the TTs in 1978 and 1979, I lived in absolute dread that something awful was going to happen to him. I didn't dare tell him, but I lived on pins while he was racing there. Even after he decided to quit, I kept my little secret from him. The danger had passed once racing had gone into history for him. He had survived all those years and fooled the fortune-teller. Who could ever have believed she was right all along and only a little bit out on her timing? And just when I was thinking that Mike and I and the kids could settle down to a life without any risks, he goes and gets killed in circumstances over which he had no control. But I'll bet he fought like a bloody demon right until the very last fraction of a second.

'That palmist did have one more forecast; she said I'd re-marry in my early forties. But I think she's going to be wrong there. Who could replace a man like Mike?'

They had first met in 1962 when Mike was well on his way to becoming a superstar in a sport that was indulgently dismissed as providing spectacle only for the working classes, with performers of lower origins than those in the four-wheeled Grand Prix racing world. He started to give it all its early glow, not merely because he was a millionaire's son, but because of his incredible talent. He was hailed, to his burning embarrassment, as the wonderboy of motor-cycle racing, and he was headlined as such not only in Britain but abroad too. Even if his father, Stan, had spent twice as much money as he did, he could not have turned Mike into a racer of such startling quality unless the talent was already there.

This was the atmosphere in which Pauline found herself in early summer at Snetterton, the homely little circuit in

Mike

East Anglia, when she accompanied a group of friends to the races. Mike, with his expansive back-up team, was dominating the paddock scene. The racer whom Pauline and her friends had gone to support was an also-ran who was having plenty of trouble with his bike. The plugs kept oiling up and Pauline was dared to go over and ask Mike, who had a vanload of spares, if he could find some plugs he would not need to help out.

'He was in the back of the van when I arrived. The great man ... the star ... with everybody staring in. It must have been terrible for him, but he didn't show it. The van's walls were covered in rather-rude pin-ups of nude girls, all that *Playboy* centre-fold stuff. I thought they were a bit cheeky.

'And suddenly there he was standing in front of me, wondering what the hell I wanted. An autograph, I suppose. Anyway, I asked him if he had any plugs to spare for a friend of mine and without any question he grabbed some out of a box and handed them over. And he wouldn't take any money. I thought he was quite lovely, especially for such a big star. There was no edge to him. And certainly no vanity.

'I watched him race, of course, and he was fabulous and I was quite thrilled by it all. But I didn't see him again until much later in the summer, June in fact, at the TT. And he was the real big star there, of course.

'The day before I was due to go home I was strolling through the paddock area and I spotted him sitting on the grass, surrounded, as usual, by a great gang of people. I must have looked a fine sight! I was totally inappropriately dressed for the races. I was wearing an ever-so-tight little mini-skirt and high-heel shoes and finding it difficult to do anything other than wobble along, really. Can you imagine?

'I was sure he had not noticed me and I walked on without saying anything or giving away that I had seen him. But he came after me and said: "Hello, you old ratbag. How are you doing? What about coming out with me tonight?" Just like that. Typically cheeky, but full of good humour, and utterly irresistible. I was delighted and flattered. Getting a date with him – the *big star* – was fantastic. Everybody was after him. I had nothing to wear, so I had to rush around Douglas to buy some gear. And I was outside the Villa Marina, the place where they have all the big prize presentations for the races, at dead on seven o'clock. But there was no sign of him.

'It got to 7.15 and still no sign and I thought the big star had stood me up. But I decided to give him another fifteen minutes. It was awful. All the other girls were walking by with their fellas and everybody was happy and having a good time and there was I like a big wallflower waiting for the most desirable and attractive man on the island. Then, in the distance, coming down the long hill from Onchan Head where he was staying at the Douglas Bay Hotel, I could see his flashy white Jaguar speeding in my direction. Of course, the date was not until 7.30 and I'd got the time wrong. Unpunctuality to Mike was the biggest sin of them all – as I found out later – and he was right on time.

'We went to the pictures and saw a film, prophetically called *A Kind of Loving*. Very romantic. And he was just lovely to be with – but then we didn't meet up again for ages and ages. Five years. He was living in Oxford with his mother and father and I was miles away in Essex. In the meantime I'd got myself married and Mike was away racing all the time – but then he came back into my life in the strangest way.

'He had a lovely black girlfriend called Irma and by coincidence she was a friend of mine who used to come into the hairdressers I worked at in Kensington. One day she asked me if I'd like to go along with her to Brands Hatch to watch her boyfriend racing, a boy called Mike! She kept going on about him, how super he was and what a big star he was in racing. I didn't let on, but it was plain to me it was the same Mike and she certainly didn't need to tell me how smashing he was. I already knew. But I dared not tell her, she was crazy about him. Anyway, I agreed to go along. Not that it took much persuasion!

'I was completely different from the last time he had seen me and I didn't think he'd recognise me at all. My hair was longer and I was no longer the green little country girl up from the sticks and impressed by the big time! I had been a

Mike

model, an actress and an air stewardess in the time in between and I was a different girl, far more sophisticated.

'It wasn't until after the racing, when we were all having a few drinks, that he suddenly remembered who I was and he kept pestering me for my telephone number. I was thinking about Irma – anyway, she'd have taken a contract out on me, I'm sure, if she'd seen what was going on – and I resisted. But then Mike's pal, Bill Ivy, threw a party at his place near Brands and a whole crowd of us stayed the night. The next morning I gave Bill my phone number as I left for home and within two days, of course, up came the telephone call.

' "It's Mike," said the voice.
' "Mike who?"
' "Hailwood, you nutcase."
' "How did you get my number?"
' "Ah, I have my little spies and informers."

'He had ladies all over the world and I fully understood how attractive he was to them. Everybody loves a winner, or wants to. And I didn't even think about his umpteen thousand women. I just loved him getting in touch with me again. Irma wasn't too happy and she was extremely angry when she found out, but I reasoned I had known him a long time before she did and that I wouldn't feel guilty because I was only reclaiming somebody I had already fallen for. The three of us used to go out night-clubbing occasionally afterwards and Mike would dance with her, but staying well within my sight as if to say "Look what a good boy I am these days."

'I was divorced early in 1968, but as Mike had always stressed he would not get married, I never used to think too much about being wed again. Just so long as we were together I was happy and content. Being a wife was not all that important to me, though I often thought it would be very nice to be married to Mike.

'Then we moved to South Africa and it looked as if we would be staying there for ever. I applied for residency papers because we had our lovely house near Durban, Mike had a house-building business going, everything in the garden seemed rosy, and this seemed to be the right way to

Pauline's Story, and More ...

go about becoming a permanent stayer. But the authorities refused to grant me the papers unless I was wed – and they succeeded in making me feel guilty and rotten that I was living with Mike without being married to him. I went home and told him my feelings and he saw how upset I was. "Right," he said, "we'll get married then." Just like that. That was his proposal! I couldn't believe what I'd heard after listening to him for ages vowing he'd never get wed. And how romantic! I don't think! But here was Hailwood going against all his principles and proposing marriage. "We might as well," he said. "You'd better make the arrangements." And nothing more was said for ages. I didn't like to go on to him about it in case he had a change of heart.

'We returned to England and did the job at Maidenhead Registry Office. But before we got there, I said to him "Are you sure you want to go through with this?" I still couldn't believe it – but I thought I'd better get him hooked while he was still in the mood. It was all kept a big secret and he only mentioned it to a friend in America, and he was so stunned by the news that he got on a plane right away and flew in to be a witness. I don't think he could believe his own eyes and ears even when he was standing with us in front of the registrar.

'But the old Hailwood was still lurking. He left me to honeymoon on my own! He and a couple of friends, a film-maker called John Tully and the German driver Jochen Mass, had bought a huge ship – the sister to the 'Onedin Line' ship, the *Charlotte-Rose*, used in the television series – and were going into business with tourist cruises either around the South of France or in the Caribbean. She was called *Aquilla-Marina* and was really beautiful and superbly appointed, and it was hoped they could grab some dollars from rich American holidaymakers with a crew dressed up as pirates.

'Straight after the wedding Mike went off racing in France – Dijon, I think – but failed to come home afterwards. And I had no idea where he'd gone. But what he'd done was he had slipped down to the South of France, where the ship was based, without telling me, and had gone off cruising with his

Mike

mates. In the meantime I was honeymooning all alone.

'I hadn't a clue as to his whereabouts until I got a phone call from the airport. It was Mike saying "Come and collect me at Heathrow." I was blazing and drove to the airport fully intent on giving him a blast, but when I saw him all tanned and fit, looking so fantastic in his tight white pants, I forgave him everything. And we were both in a mood to make it a memorable honeymoon!

'Mike's interest in the venture closed when it started to cost huge amounts of money, far more than he was prepared to spend. And he had already pumped a small fortune into it. Then they had bad luck with their captains. They didn't seem to be able to choose the right ones for the ship – they kept on clouting the walls of the harbour at Villefranche and it didn't go down too well with the authorities. I think Prince Rainier had granted them special permission to sail in and out of Monaco as their base headquarters, all because of his long-standing admiration for Grand Prix racing drivers and what they had done over the years for his principality. But it all went flat for Mike and he sold out his share, and I was glad. It was all a big drain on his money, even if it was fun for a while.'

Ironically, for all his magnificent organisational ability and cool thinking, his clear but hard-headed approach to money matters, and his driving ambitions to do well at whatever he attempted, Mike was never a success in business matters, even though he felt the need for investment. It was one trait which he did not inherit from his father, who was a brilliantly astute businessman who made a million and more from a string of motor-bike shops that ranged from one end of Britain to the other. Mike flirted, maybe a little too casually, with various projects: one was an air-taxi service, though he never finished his flying lessons after getting a trainer-plane into an enormous skid on the runway, and then hair-raisingly touching power-cables when he and his old friend and Honda team-mate, Jim Redman, were landing near Manchester *en route* to Oulton Park. Other projects were executive house-building in Durban, villa rentals in the Bahamas, his motor-bike firm

Pauline's Story, and More ...

with Rod Gould and, strangest of all, a prawn farm in South Africa. But he did not know anything about *that* until a man acting for him revealed he had invested a lump of Mike's money, without permission, in the business. It was a move that so angered Mike that he sued the man for the return of the cash.

'I have a special ability,' he once told me, 'to get into businesses that let me down and to buy houses when the market is up and to sell when it is down. No matter how I try, I can't seem to reverse the trend. It's a special gift. It's called stupidity.' Once, when he was trying to sell a house, and the market was sky-high and buyers were a rare breed, he loaned a man the money to purchase the house. Again, when he couldn't be bothered with all the rigmarole of mortages, after listening to an estate agent and a lawyer droning on about interest rates, percentages, valuations and all the other mumbo-jumbo that goes with it, he stopped them short by pulling out his cheque book and paying cash. It was the same sudden, impulsive burst of impatience that once provoked him into tossing a troublesome television set out of his fourth-storey apartment window – then ringing the rental company to collect what was left of it from the pavement below and, at the same time, leaving a cheque to cover the cost of a replacement.

Generally, however, Mike's nature was the embodiment of calm rationale, carefully considered action and decisive response – not only on the race track, but in life too. It was a standard he automatically lived by and one which caused his old Grand Prix adversary Jackie Stewart to say of him:

'Mike was a real slow burner. His action in pulling Clay Regazzoni to safety in South Africa showed that. He always seemed to have the knack of being able to do what was necessary without any spectacular intent and I have always been impressed by men who react like that.

'I didn't see any of what went on when he rescued Clay and he didn't stay around to talk about it. I was too busy trying to win; I knew something had happened behind me, but I didn't know how serious it was, because when I came round I could see there had been a shunt and a fire. But it did

Mike

not surprise me at all when I was told what Mike had done in saving the fellow's life and putting his own very much at risk. It just seemed to me that if anybody was capable of such action, it was old Hailwood. He wouldn't even consider the danger if he knew he was in a position to do something to help.'

Close as I was to Mike and much as he often confided his innermost thoughts and personal secrets to me, he never, ever talked about the actions that earned him the George Medal, one of the highest awards for bravery that can be bestowed on anybody outside the Services. I tried often enough, but he shrugged off any attempt to get him to open up about it – and when he was confronted by Regazzoni on television after he had been tricked into being the subject of a *This is Your Life* programme, he visibly winced with embarrassment.

Mike's courage had faced its sternest confrontation at Kyalami in the 1973 South African Grand Prix, yet he had not shirked the challenge. When, on the third lap, Regazzoni collided with Belgian ace Jackie Ickx and another driver, Mike, chasing hard, sideswiped the wreckage. As his car came to a halt, he clambered out and immediately saw that the Swiss driver, Regazzoni, was still trapped and his car was a raging inferno. Mike had been showered with petrol and his overalls were ablaze, but he punched a marshal who tried to stop him and plunged into the fire to haul Reggazoni clear. Mike got burned himself, but there was never any thought in his mind for his own safety. His code was simple; a man was in danger of losing his life and Mike was in a position to save him. The whole dramatic episode was filmed by a long-focus television camera, not terribly clearly, but enough to show Mike's fearsome determination not to let Regazzoni die. I only saw it years afterwards and it was quite the most astonishing act of bravery I had ever watched. You would have thought Regazzoni was a goner and you would have thought, too, that nobody could have been expected to put his own life on the line to dive into the flames to the rescue. It would have been a severe test for a rescue expert geared up for the job; for a man like Mike, dressed only in

Pauline's Story, and More ...

overalls which quickly caught fire, it was an act of supreme courage.

It was a tragedy that Regazzoni should survive that particular nightmare only to suffer another crash that left him a cripple confined to a wheelchair. I saw him at Imola, Italy, in 1983, ten years after Mike's lifesaving rescue, and his appreciation of the Hailwood brand of action was still as warm.

He was a very sad figure, wheeling his way along the Imola paddock. But he smiled hugely at the memory of the man who had risked his life for him. 'It was so brave of Mike,' he said, 'and there is no doubt I owe him my life.'

Pauline was at the race that day, but she had no idea what had gone on. Mike certainly did not tell her. And she only found out what had happened a day later when she opened the papers and saw the whole drama spread across the front pages ...

'I can recall vividly,' she told me,' that Mike came walking up the pit lane and he looked terrible, worse than I'd ever seen him look all the time I had known him. He was tight-lipped, drawn and ashen-faced. And he was more than a bit anxious to get away from the place. In fact, he was very agitated about leaving and couldn't wait, so we got on the bike we'd come on and went home. And in total silence too. I thought he must have had one really big hairy moment and didn't want to talk about it. I thought he must have scared himself so much he just wanted to forget.

'As soon as we got into the house, he disappeared for a bath. Afterwards we had a couple of drinks and settled down for a nice relaxing evening on our own. He still didn't want to open up about what it was that was obviously troubling him and he was always best left to his own devices in those circumstances, so I didn't push for any answers even though I had never seen him quite so shaken.

'The next morning the papers arrived and I was staggered to see what he had done. I read about it, and I still couldn't believe what my eyes were seeing in black and white in front of me. But there it was. Mike had seen Clay's predicament. A marshal was standing there doing nothing, apparently

Mike

having given up any hope for Clay's chances. But not my Mike. In he went and he only came out when his clothes caught fire. He doused them out and went in again. This time he managed to haul big old Clay to safety.

'When I said to him, "Jesus, I don't believe it. You did all that and you never even mentioned it to me," he just replied, "Firemen do it every day." And that was that. He wouldn't elaborate except to add "It was nothing special."

'I tried hard, but he would not tell me more. He refused steadfastly and was plainly not happy with all the coverage it had been given in the papers and the spotlight that had naturally fallen on him. Later, he received a letter from Clay – but even when I sneaked a look at it I couldn't understand what it said because it was in Italian, a language Mike understood and spoke very well. When I asked him to tell me what Clay had written he refused. Mike considered it his own affair and a totally private communication between him and Regazzoni, and there was no way I could break in. I was tingling with excitement and pride at what Mike had done. But it was typical of him to keep it all under wraps.

'It was the same when he was in pain. He never used to moan about it or make a fuss. He kept it all locked up inside and didn't want to trouble anybody else or worry them with his own problems which he always considered trivial. He never bemoaned his luck – not even when that big shunt at the Nürburgring put an end to his car-racing career. He suffered terrible agonies for ages afterwards, was in pain for much of the time, but never let on and never harped on about it. It was to him part and parcel of the job – he just wanted to get on with the job of getting as fit and healthy as he could as quickly as possible and he went through agonies to do it.'

I saw this attitude at close range during his TT comeback in 1978. He scared us all in the team by falling off a 250cc Yamaha in the morning of the extremely important afternoon's Formula One world championship race. A new front tyre had not scrubbed in sufficiently and as he leaned into Braddan and flicked the bike over, it suddenly slid away and pitched him over the top.

Pauline's Story, and More ...

I went to collect him to bring him back to the grandstand area and he was quite shaken; it was his first TT tumble for years and it had to happen on the morning of his dramatic return to racing on the island. But worse, he had burst his fingers and only admitted it when I noticed the blood seeping through his gloves. He refused to go to hospital for a check, he didn't want to panic anybody that he might have to miss the race. Even though he was in a lot of pain from his injured fingers throughout the gruelling six-lap event, there was no thought in his head of either quitting or complaining. The handshakes at the end of the race were extremely painful affairs.

Jackie Stewart recalls that he used to call him 'Micycle the Bicycle' and adds: 'He was so much fun and such a charismatic individual it was clear to me why he enjoyed such enormous popularity. That incredible shyness in a man of his phenomenal success made him so appealing – the ladies were crazy about him. Men, too, liked him tremendously. But through it all Mike just kept on being his normal, natural self, happy with the world, feeling good to be alive and determined to enjoy every minute of it. And, boy, did he!

'The interesting point about him was that he was not like, say, Barry Sheene, one of those accelerated media personalities whose trendy, topical looks give him a wider fame than his achievements probably deserve. Mike was the amazing product of an era when coverage of his sport on television and in the newspapers was primitive, to say the least. But what he stood for and the way he went about it with such tremendous success and style gave him his charisma, and this was recognised by the media all those years ago, even if they did not spread it across the pages of the papers as they did much later. For me, that makes Mike's appeal even more remarkable; he wasn't being pushed and promoted like the stars who came long after him but he was bigger than any of them ever could be.

'We did not spend all that much time together. I was going through a particularly high-energy period of my life and career and was being pulled here, there and everywhere. But

Mike

when we did get together, maybe at his old pal Paddy Driver's ranch down in South Africa, or with any of his chums, it was obvious to me that he was only really happy and content when he was surrounded by familiar faces and mates and mostly his motor-cycle race gang. He felt that guys who raced cars were a wee bit too snobbish for him. It was a falsehood, really, and he was quite wrong. They may have been a bit stand-offish with him because he had come as the great big star into their world and, maybe, some of them were a little cautious, maybe a bit too wary, and he couldn't get close enough to them to find out they were quite okay. He was the rich guy with the millionaire father and, I think, guys in my sport were waiting for him to show his hand so they could get to work him out. But Mike never really gave my people a chance, and it was a pity because they would have loved him as much as I did if they had only been given the opportunity to get close enough to him to find out what made him tick.

'I knew enough motor-cycle racers to know how they behaved and what sort of guys they were underneath. Bob McIntyre, for instance, was a great pal. An absolute gentleman who, like Mike, never projected himself in any deliberate way. Mike, we all knew, was the superstar in his own field – but now he was in ours and it was a whole lot different for him.

'The contrast to his rather reserved attitude was his best pal, little Bill Ivy. He came in like a tornado, a man considerably less sophisticated than Mike. But people in the car world all loved him right away. He just mixed in straight away and got down to the business of putting himself around. Mike couldn't help the way he was, but I don't think he ever really put himself out to give us time to work him out. It was typical, I suppose, that his best friend became Denny Hulme, a man with no razzmatazz, a super nice guy devoid of bullshit and pretence, and Mike loved bumming around with him. They were perfect mates.

'It was no big surprise to any of us on the Grand Prix scene that the two of them, both men unfussed by the highly charged atmosphere of Formula One, should turn out to be

Pauline's Story, and More ...

such big pals. Neither was any sort of a poser, both were down-to-earth, and each of them appreciated the other's incredible talent.'

Stewart is an unashamed admirer of Mike and held him in high regard as a race-car driver, an accolade which few people who knew no better were prepared to grant to the man who had switched from two wheels to four in the hope that he could emulate his friend John Surtees, who was the only man to have clinched world titles in both categories.

'When Mike was on form, he was bloody good,' said Stewart, 'but he was not always on top form. Maybe it was because for a long time in his Formula One career he had equipment that was not as good as it might have been for a man of his natural skill and undoubted talent. Later on, when he was with Yardley-McLaren, he showed what he was capable of producing when he had a good car, and he made one or two people sit up and take notice. He had some tremendous drives – and some awful luck. That bad crash at the Nürburgring, for instance. That was terrible and it put him out of racing. It was doubly tragic because at the time he was getting his act together.'

In fact Mike, thirty-three that year, was enjoying a soaring confidence in Formula One. Loyalty to his old friend had kept him plugging away in the Surtees team, which really he should have left long before he did. But when he finally split, there were four other teams in the chase for his signature, and Yardley-McLaren won it. Almost immediately it could be seen that at long last he had a car that was as good as his ambitions and aims demanded. At one stage of the 1974 season, driving at his absolute best, he was running fifth in the drivers' championship after the Brazilian and Argentine Grands Prix, the highest-placed British driver, and he was improving and getting faster with every race.

He might just have got that little bit closer to equalling his old boss John Surtees's record double on titles had he not been unlucky enough to crash so disastrously at the West German Grand Prix when he was running fourth and pulling in the third man.

'Brain fade,' he said, 'that was the cause. Pure and simple.

Mike

I just lost my concentration and went straight on at about 180 miles-an-hour. And the quickest way I know to stop is to hit the armco. I came to a dead stop in about twenty feet and I knew it was going to hurt. It certainly did.

'I was lucky I wasn't guillotined. When I came round this bloody big hooter of mine was pressed right up against the metal of the barrier. My right leg, the one that does all the work in a racing car, was shattered in three places. My ankle was a jelly of crushed bones and it seemed to take years before they cut me free. I was lucky to be alive, though, and I was grateful for that much,' he told me later.

He went on: 'But I told myself even then that I wasn't going to stop racing.' It was the first big fight Mike had faced that he failed to win. For despite his immense determination, long hours of treatment and physiotherapy at Stoke Mandeville hospital, journeys through the pain barrier every day, he was never in a position to race cars again. A £650 insurance premium he had paid at the start of the season looked after the massive medical bills, but it couldn't cure his crankiness at knowing inwardly he was finished as a Grand Prix car driver, and he faced the rest of his life trying to master a heavy limp. His Formula One career closed without him ever winning a Grand Prix, though he had come tantalisingly close with a second place in a stirring finish at Monza's Italian Grand Prix.

That was in 1972, his most successful year, when he shadowed the eventual world champion Emerson Fittipaldi's Lotus Ford across the line in his Surtees Ford. Racing luminaries like Denny Hulme, Peter Revson, Graham Hill, Peter Gethin and Jackie Ickx were all outclassed that day in September.

At the other end of the year, March, he had set the fastest lap in the 79-lap South African Grand Prix at Kyalami, scene one year later of his stirring rescue. He had bettered even the maestro Jackie Stewart – but it was his firmest race friend Denny Hulme who clinched victory with Emerson Fittipaldi next and Peter Revson third. When it came to the final count-up Mike was in eighth position in the championship; behind him were men of the high calibre of Ronnie Peterson,

Pauline's Story, and More ...

Graham Hill, Mario Andretti, Carlos Reutemann, de Adamich, Brian Redman, Ganley, Pace and Gethin. It was a vast improvement on his 1971 placing of eighteenth with only three title points scored. And, up to the time he had to quit because of the West German Grand Prix pile-up, he was bidding for a high place among the top three. In 1974 he finished up with fourteen championship points, enough to keep him in tenth position, shared with the Belgian star Ickx, despite completing only ten Grands Prix that season before the crash. He had been fourth at Buenos Aires in the Argentine Grand Prix in January, fifth one week later at Interlagos, Brazil, third in the 78-lap South African, then he hit a run of bad luck until he got back into the points at Zandvoort with a fifth place in the sand-blasted Dutch Grand Prix. His feeling that he had turned the corner, as it were, was exploded in that mysterious fourth-lap crash which nearly killed him and which most certainly brought a halt to a career enjoying a spectacular upturn.

In fifty Grands Prix in ten years his record was one second place (Italy, 1972), one third (South Africa, 1974), five fourth places (Italy, 1971; Belgium and Austria, 1972; Argentina and Holland, 1974), one fifth place (Brazil, 1974) and two sixths (Monaco, 1964, and France, 1972). In 1964 he was 19th with one point; in 1971 he was 18th with 3 points; in 1972 he was 8th with 13 points; and in 1974 10th with 12 points. He spent five laps in the lead in races and just once set up the fastest lap. These statistics cloak a colourful background of dramas, crashes, and freaks, like the time his helmet worked loose and the chin guard rode up over his eyes as he was on an outside line and overtaking in the Spanish Grand Prix, breakdowns of machinery not equal to his ambitions, and more incidents, good and bad, at one circuit – Kyalami – that any one driver ever deserved. 'That place is all things to me,' he once said. 'I can't seem to race there without something happening.'

Jackie Stewart would testify to Mike's dash at the South African venue. He was powering through a long bend, fairly confident that nobody else could get through there quite as fast and, I suppose, a little more relaxed than he would

Mike

normally be, when the front wheel of another car began to inch its way into his vision in the corner of his eye the car began to assume shape and colour. Of course, it was Mike, overtaking where nobody else would dare challenge the master; I can imagine the huge grin under that red, white and gold helmet as he nosed past the champion.

When word flew around the pit lane that Mike had set up the quickest time at Kyalami his response was: 'Not bad, eh? And I didn't get to bed until four o'clock this morning.'

'Mike was always ready to take up the fringe benefits, shall we say,' said Dickie Attwood. 'He was famed for it; I don't know how he found the energy to race! But it was part of his character, and we loved him for his devil-may-care stance.'

Attwood, one of Mike's oldest allies, a Le Mans 24-hour race winner in 1970 and a runner-up in 1971, was treated to a typical bout of Hailwood mischief even before they met.

'We must have met in Formula Junior,' said Dickie, 'because we were in it at the same time. But I can't remember meeting him at all; perhaps it was because I hadn't come under his close scrutiny. I certainly did, however, in 1965 when I was getting ready for the Monaco Grand Prix.

'BRM had me on contract for two years as a test and development driver, but I wasn't getting any racing done and that didn't please me at all. Ritchie Ginther was the star boy and he, of course, was getting all the treatment. When I complained about it they said they would give me an engine with which to do as I wanted. Well, I came to an agreement with the Reg Parnell team – they were bloody glad to have me along. After all, I had a full works engine, a real good one too. So we put it in one of their cars and it became the BRM-Parnell-Lotus. Mike was already in the team; he'd done everything he could on bikes and he wanted to try his hand in cars so, rather foolishly I thought, he sank a good deal of money into the Parnell team.

'He can't have been too pleased when I came along. I must have been everything he disliked. I was the successful car racer, a works-supported driver with a super BRM engine to put into the Parnell-Lotus when he had to struggle on as best

Pauline's Story, and More ...

he could, and here I was, coming into his little world, all snooty and snobbish.

'I went along to Parnell HQ at Arundel for a fitting before the 1965 Monaco Grand Prix. Mike wasn't there, he'd already left. But he'd left his mark. All over the car there were stickers – 'gear stick', 'brake', 'steering wheel', 'rev counter' – I didn't really understand what it all meant.

'But it was merely Mike's way of taking the mickey out of this poofter car racer, the man who was everything he really wanted to be, a bit fussed over and given most of the things he wanted in full works style. And then when we met at Monaco he used to tease me something horrible; I suffered, but it was all in fun. It was only when I managed to get sixth fastest in practice, and he was struggling near the back and feeling very downhearted, that he realised I could drive a bit as well. After that, and right after the race, we became the best of friends. We were whooping like madmen, drunk as idiots, and driving through Monte Carlo at four o'clock in the morning with our girlfriends. We just hit it off and never looked back.

'It's not surprising really, when I look back, that he might have been a bit bitter and jealous. His car was such an old banger, and he was having to battle so hard and so frustratingly, and mine was that much quicker and I had a much easier time. But once we had broken the barriers down, we were okay.'

Attwood, a wealthy businessman on a par with Mike, plainly had nothing to gain from him, only a deep and lasting kinship, and it was a point that was always uppermost in Mike's mind when so many around him had cheated him, ripped him off or used him to their own financial advantage.

'It's a great sadness', said Attwood, 'that Mike never really knew all the people who wanted to know him for himself. He was forced to be suspicious because so many so-called mates had ripped him off. That made him stand-offish and he regarded a lot of people as merely hangers-on who wanted to get out of him what they could. In many cases it was an accurate judgement. But in others it

Mike

was wide of the mark. With his true friends he worked really hard and he was a most constant mate; he made everything that much brighter when he was around. His outrageousness was legendary and, provided he was having fun and doing nobody any harm, he was happy.

'Whatever jealousies there were could only have been about his incredible talent and success – he could never have upset people by harping on it all. He made so light of it.

'I admired his attitude totally. He just could not be bothered if he didn't like the way things were going; he'd just say "bollocks" to it and move on elsewhere. He'd go back to where he could get help, or fun, or anything else that would bring his life back into the order he liked it to be. He was so light-hearted about everything it was infectious; it was bloody hard to be serious when he was around. He took his racing seriously enough, on bikes and in cars, but after the race was over, it was party-time.

'He probably had his best time in cars in Formula 5000, even though he had rubbish motors to deal with. He always said it was great fun and he put every ounce of effort into it, and he had a good deal of satisfaction out of it. Formula One was a whole world different to him. He was certainly as quick as anybody else around, he could perform okay, but he was absolutely useless technically. His know-how on setting up a car was virtually nil. Graham Hill had a little black book full of hints and tips and painstakingly recorded details about circuit conditions, and he tried to help Mike all he could, but it made little difference. A car is such an individual piece of equipment you had to sort it out yourself. It was all too much of a complicated puzzle for him.

'The upshot was that Mike had to rely a lot on his skill, rather than his experience and technical expertise – that's a laugh – to get himself out of tight spots. He didn't seem to think too far ahead in that respect; he was happy to use his instincts and that incredible natural ability and daring to get him through. I don't think he was all that much better with bikes either, but they didn't take quite so much setting-up and he was such a genius on two wheels it didn't seem to make any odds at all to him that something might not be

Pauline's Story, and More ...

entirely correct on the machine. His ability was more than enough to compensate.

'In a 1000-kilometre race at the Nürburgring his big Gulf-Mirage sports car stopped and left him absolutely baffled. Afterwards, when the mechanics had taken a look round, he was told the fuel pump had jammed. Then, when he was asked why he didn't open the bonnet and give the pump a bash, he said, "I don't even know how to get the lid up, let alone work out that it was the fuel pump that was the problem."

'I can remember when I won Le Mans in 1970. Mike and his pal David Hobbs were partners in the Gulf-Mirage-Wyer 917 and there was an incredible number of accidents. Mike was among them – he went flying off the road in the wet and wrecked the car and when he walked back to the pits, looking very disconsolate indeed, his boss John Wyer shouted the immortal words "Don't ring us, we'll ring you." He was upset for a while, but he soon got over it.'

When it was revealed that Mike was going to race at the 1978 Isle of Man TT, the announcement provoked enormous interest, not just amongst bikers everywhere, but also amongst the many friends Mike had made since turning his hand to racing cars.

Dickie Attwood recalls: 'I'd never seen him race bikes, because I was away doing my thing in cars, so when he decided to make his TT comeback I knew it was something I couldn't afford to miss. I just had to be there. It was the same with Denny Hulme. He flew from New Zealand to watch. And Jim Redman. When he heard Mike was coming back, he got on the first plane he could from South Africa. Harvey Postlethwaite and Peter Warr from Walter Wolf's Grand Prix team borrowed Walter's helicopter and flew in. And so did thousands of people. None of us could have imagined in our wildest dreams that the old bugger was going to give us the treat of a lifetime, but really we should have known.'

3

TT 1978

It was a chilly May evening and Mike and I, in a 3500 Rover borrowed from an Isle of Man garage, were diving into one of the scariest sections of the TT course, the bottom of Barregarrow, a little short of 13 miles from the start, and I was convinced I was about to draw my last breath. There seems to be hardly enough room to jog between the pavement and the hedgerows with any safety and when the bump at the base of the drop, taken very quickly indeed, propels you in what seems to be one bound to the other side of the road at nearly 100 mph you feel certain the odds favour the Grim Reaper. I just shut my eyes and hoped that Mike, sitting in total calm behind the wheel, had not taken leave of his senses. But with an enviable calm which went nowhere near dissolving my apprehensions – I usually trusted his skill implicitly – he threw this mass of groaning metal and moaning Macauley into a sort of hop and skip and powered on and up out of the bend. I could not believe I had survived. I asked him, with reasonable firmness, to take me back.

He said: 'Why, do you want to do it again?'

And I said: 'No, there's a pub down the road and I want to

wait there while you practise your death-defying technique.'

'Death-defying! Don't be so bloody soft,' he said. 'I knocked it off a bit in deference to your ... shall we say ... sensitivities. I could have gone through there much quicker. No problem.'

It was, I suppose, from that very moment that the TT 1978 came alive for me. Having set the whole business of Mike's comeback into motion, I hadn't been able to assess just how serious it was to be, until we took our first fast look at the course in that early four-wheeled rehearsal for the frenetic two-wheeled activity that was to follow, when official practice began. If nobody else believed it, Mike was set in deadly determination. Not only to do well – but to win. And win in some considerable style.

He would only venture the view that he would do well even to finish – and to end up on the leader board was as much, he said, as he could expect. Secretly, despite his denials that he would have been terribly disappointed not to win at least one of the four races I had entered him for, he lived and thrived on bursts of adrenalin in the privacy of his hotel room, and on the hope that he would take a TT title to add to the twelve he had already won. Up front he laughed off suggestions that a win was a foregone conclusion; even a place in the top three, he said, was far more than he could expect. If he was fooling anybody, he was not fooling himself. We pored over the form of his rivals, discussed their chances, their TT pedigree, and their back-up and personal ambition; he looked at them whenever he could in practice and weighed up their determination, and we built up a dossier of their strengths and weaknesses and assessed them over long dinners and quieter private get-togethers out of the public gaze. And he knew, he just knew, that he could make the fairy tale come true. But he would never admit it outside the two of us; he would only say he felt a lot of pressure and responsibility both to Yamaha and Ducati and to his sponsors, Martini, who had plunged in with a lot of money.

'I don't want to let anybody down,' he told me. 'I know I can put up a good show, and maybe win one race, but most

Mike

of all I don't want anybody to be disappointed or to feel cheated. That's why I'd much rather keep the whole business low key.' But that was an impossibility.

Suddenly the bookings for the Isle of Man shot up to new levels, levels they had not reached since Mike last raced over the famous island course eleven years before. Media pressures, too, were enormous. Television, radio, magazines and newspapers from all over the world courted him on his return to racing, and he bore it all with patience and fortitude and with a happy regard for the job they were trying to do.

He was deadly serious about the whole business, and had set about getting fit for this most dramatic event with frightening ferocity and grim determination. Twelve thousand miles away in New Zealand, removed by half a world from the frantic action surrounding his comeback, Mike set about reducing his pot-belly and cutting his weight by something like twenty pounds. Out went his favourite vodka and lemonade, and the teetotal Hailwood pounded mile after mile, despite his wobbly leg, through the countryside around his lovely home, and drove himself through the stamina barrier with gruelling sessions in his swimming pool. He had always enjoyed a basic fitness, a splendid physique and an awesome single-mindedness that gave him an edge to his determination, at a time of life when he might have thought he could afford not to make such strenuous efforts; but he knew he *had* to be fit to undertake the job ahead. The TT is not a playground; the Isle of Man is a demanding $37\frac{3}{4}$-mile road course, a maze of pitfalls and an easy trap for the unwary and the unfit – it has to be treated with the very greatest respect. And he knew it. Not only that, he set about making sure that whatever tests it could throw at him, he would be equal to and capable of mastering them.

The difference between the Mike I had seen onto the plane to New Zealand after we had set up the deal, and the one who arrived at my home in the North of England, *en route* to the most stirring return to racing two weeks later, was enormous. The cheeks had hollowed; the waistline which had developed a girdle from good living was trim again; his shoulders, his forearms and his chest seemed massive and the double chin was now a firm jawline. His eyes were crystal bright and he positively exuded health, confidence and determination, but he could not beat my twelve-year-old daughter Kerris in a game of reflexes. The idea was to start and stop a stop-watch on the same button by rapping it as quickly as possible with one finger, then logging the split-time difference. He had lost so many times he started to cheat – he tickled her.

It was a completely relaxed Mike who happily slept on the make-shift bed we had set up for him in my front room; he didn't want to go into the city and sleep at a big hotel. He was far happier in a house full of people and laughter, and was very much a contributor.

Before we set off for the Isle of Man we had a dinner party at home, his last chance for a booze-up because I had sorted out with him a strict regime of no drinking and early nights, which he followed as meekly but as eagerly as any man honestly determined not to let himself or anybody else down. It was a hilarious night with a lawyer, Ken Wilkinson, and his wife Margaret; a headmaster, John Morris, and his wife Pam, and neighbours Nigel Crossley and his wife Nancy, all of them people far removed from the world of racing and, therefore, different and interesting for a man of such restless curiosity as Mike. Well aware of the monkish habits he would shortly have to adopt, he swigged enthusiastically at the nearest bottle at hand – a deeply rich vintage port. He thought, in the flickering candlelight and amidst the heady, laugh-in atmosphere, that it was rather a strong dinner red and attacked it with gusto; but he suffered the next day. We could not work out why he was so hung-over until we traced it to the port and realised he had been drinking the wrong stuff.

The Wilkinsons had made a return invitation to dinner at their home, twenty-five miles away in the lovely Lancashire countryside, and Mike was looking forward to it, but he could not lift his head and his eyes looked like rubies. 'You go,' he said. 'I'll baby-sit for you.' Hailwood, baby-sitter!

Mike

We left him with a tube of aspirin, a dimmed light and the television turned down to a gentle, far-off murmur – but he was happy to relieve us of the responsibility of looking after him. When we returned home at 2 am he had even washed the dishes.

'If I didn't know you were on my side,' he said, 'I'd be convinced you were trying to nobble me before the TT. I'll bet you're in Gerald Davison's pay,' he laughed.

Davison, from Honda, had apparently said that he had turned Mike down for a TT ride, even though we had never approached him, and he became a standing, long-running joke between us. He seemed to us to have got rather the wrong end of the stick, and he amused us both so much we used to make up nicknames for him. 'Oliver' was the most popular because it fitted as a middle initial; then 'Gainsborough' because we would quite often see him about the place in the brightest Honda regalia, a dazzling advertisement for the company, wearing a sort of American Admiral-of-the-Fleet baseball cap dappled with gold braid on the peak. There was a showy peacock quality to the Honda team that year.

In contrast to the massive Honda back-up for Phil Read in the Isle of Man, Mike's Ducati support was positively impoverished; but we knew we had the best man. And that was what counted; nothing that Davison or the Honda millions or even Read, a great rider, could do would take that away. And while there may have been quite natural doubts about Mike's ability to step straight back into the fray and do anything other than register a reasonable placing, we in the team knew that his own pride and determination would settle for nothing less than a win and a wipe-out of the Honda champion Read, his old Grand Prix adversary. Davison's feelings that Mike would not beat Read, the winner the year before, were about to be rammed convincingly down his throat – but Mike, despite the intensity of his build-up and the anger he felt at the Honda attitude, refused to be tricked into any boastful remarks. Whatever he felt, he kept his feelings strictly within the privacy of our own conversations, and let others get on with the

TT 1978

loose-tongued stupidity of men who were more hot air than good substance. And there *were* serious doubters.

I do not suppose there was anybody connected in even the remotest way with the TT who failed to appreciate the massive, world-wide interest which Mike's reappearance as a rider at the Isle of Man had created. He was like a life-giving injection in a body fast becoming drained of its vitality. Even so, he insisted:

'I just hope people don't expect too much from me. I will try my best, but it would be impossible for me to be anything like I was when I last raced the place eleven years ago. I shall try to be as competitive as I know how, but I'd be an extremely pretentious man to think that I could take up where I left off or even come close to being as effective as I was all those years ago.'

Martini had moved in to support Mike's return and they did it in the fine style one had always associated with the company. When I had fixed their sponsorship, they were quick to realise the importance of Mike's romantic return and to recognise the special quality of the man, his reputation, and his suitability to the enhancement of their product. Whenever and wherever they wanted him to appear, he was always on time, superbly turned out, correctly mannered and ready to fit into their upper-class image of what a superstar should look like holding one of their drinks in his hand. Undoubtedly they gave the whole affair a stamp of style and worldliness, and together with Mike propelled motor-cycle racing to new levels of universal acceptability. Not even Honda, for all their gaudy gear, or Marlboro, for all their media-courtship in Grand Prix racing and their ocean-going promotions yacht in support of Agostini at the TT, had managed that. Mike and Martini, despite problems with the Yamaha back-up, were a marriage that suddenly made the TT a race apart. But this is a standing it has never recaptured since.

Although I had insisted in the deals which I had struck that Mike could not be expected to win, he himself now felt it was the least he could do – and, quite suddenly, the affair became deadly serious. What had set out as a frolic had

Mike

gained such momentum that it was impossible to treat it in any way other than a bid to win, a tremendous mountain to be climbed by a man who had been missing from the scene for eleven years.

I recall sitting in deckchairs on the terrace of the Palace-Casino Hotel on Douglas Promenade. Mike was a picture of fitness and strength. Practice had not yet begun, but we had spent countless hours retracing his old lines around the up-hill-and-down-dale course in our car. We had listened to advice from sportsmen like Mick Grant and Tom Herron, men who were to be among the sternest of rivals but who were ready and happy to help all they could. And Mike said:

'Hey, it's suddenly got all serious. I didn't intend it to be like this, but now it is I'll give it my best shot. There's too much money, too much faith in me, and too many people relying on me to put up a really good show to play about any more.' And that's just how it was – but there was still a bubble of fun bursting to get out.

We had discovered that the mysterious 5ft-by-3ft hessian-covered boards on the walls in the corridor outside our hotel bedrooms shielded the workings to all the toilets and that once you had removed them you could get at the innards of the plumbing and work the lavatory flush.

There can be few things more private than a trip to the toilet and to have it suddenly flush either while you are sitting on it or even when you are a good few feet away in the bedroom can be a most alarming experience. It was, for Mike, too good an opportunity for mischief to miss and the victim was chosen – the *Daily Mirror* reporter Peter Cooper and his wife Shirley, enjoying a second honeymoon while Peter helped me.

It was pretty evident to us that they were getting warmed up to the task over dinner at the Palace – the champagne was cascading, with intertwined arms they sipped a loving-cup of bubbly, and they gazed into each other's eyes with neither sight nor thought for anybody else. And at about 10 o'clock they set off for their bedroom overlooking the twinkling lights of the seafront. After about fifteen minutes we followed them up to the third floor and got to work on removing the hessian cover from the wall beside their door. We could hear the murmur of voices inside, soft music, and waited until the strip of light under the door went out. Ten minutes. Then Mike flushed the loo – and we collapsed into a heap of giggles in the corridor. The strip of light reappeared under the door and inside, over the gushing waters of the toilet, we could hear Peter's deep Yorkshire voice: 'What the bloody 'ell's goin' on? Eh, look at this Shirley. The bloody lav's going on its own. It's gone daft.' Mike was swishing the handle up and down and it was wagging like a tail set in the tiles of Peter's bathroom; then he heard us laughing helplessly outside in the corridor.

His face was a picture of black intent when he threw open the door but what made it even funnier for us was that he was wearing only the top half of a pair of Kung-Fu pyjamas; his legs, like those of a stocky Japanese wrestler, were splayed revealingly. Shirley was in a sheer negligée, and it was obvious that their second honeymoon had been well under way when Mike flushed it away. It was for us a patent success; for Peter and Shirley, once they had got over the shock of thinking somebody was in their toilet, it was memorably funny. Though I'm not sure they ever forgave us.

Mike and I, so fevered by our huge breakthrough, spent the rest of the night prowling the corridors, lifting the hessian blocks, flushing the loos and sprinting off to the safety of our rooms to peep round the doors with tears in our eyes, looking at totally baffled guests who could not work out that phantom flushers had been at work.

It had become a drug, and it left us absolutely helpless. We did just about everybody in the hotel. But we could not crack one man, three doors away and therefore a prime target since we had a bolt-hole close at hand. What was left of the night we spent creeping to his room, flushing the lavatory and speeding off giggling to the safety of our rooms. Nothing. And we must have tried it at least six times. Still nothing. No response at all. We were terribly frustrated. We could see all the hessian blocks off the wall, right along

Mike

the corridors, and each of them had been in its own way an unqualified success. But this one was a total failure. We could not work out why. We had seen him totter along the corridor. Well dressed, slightly drunk, and a bit pompous from our experience of him in the bar. In the end we gave up.

We saw him at breakfast the next morning. We were still aching from the rather juvenile fun of it all when the fellow came into the dining room and said a polite 'Good morning'. It was only then we noticed he was wearing a hearing-aid. He must have switched it off when he went to bed. The hotel management were more than a little curious about who among their guests seemed to be suffering some sort of loo fetish: Peter and Shirley Cooper, our first-night victims, spent a nervous week trying to resume where they had left off. At least, that is what they claimed.

In the meantime the serious business of winning the TT had assumed enormous proportions. The difficulty was getting enough free time for Mike in between practice and the demands of the media, particularly TV men who were fascinated by the splendour of it all and riveted by this near-forty-year-old who was happily prepared to take on the world's finest road racers, all much younger, on the sport's most testing circuit.

Mick Grant, the man who had felt honoured to crack Mike's 1967 500cc lap record in 1975, the first year he met him, recalls: 'I thought he was tempting providence and that it was absolutely impossible, even for a man of his standing, to come back and do well, never mind win.'

Grant, a no-nonsense Yorkshireman with a colliery background, had come late into racing, and by the time he was going well, Mike had moved on into Grand Prix car racing.

'In fact,' said Grant at his home in Wakefield, 'the only time I'd come into Mike's orbit was at Silverstone in 1972. He was playing about on a 250 Yamaha, a light-hearted return to racing that came to nothing. I was motoring along very nicely when this guy came flying by. He was wearing a red helmet and nondescript leathers. No name on his back.

TT 1978

But I knew right away who it was. He went past like a rocket. It just had to be Hailwood – and I never saw him again in the race after that. He finished sixth, I think. And he was only messing about! Incredible.

'So when I heard he was coming back to the TT in '78 I was really excited. The idea of taking him on at the island, a place that had been a happy hunting ground for me, was marvellous. I knew he had a hard job in front of him, not only from my point of view, but there was Read, John Williams, Tom Herron, Charlie Williams, all TT specialists and top-class road racers, and he had been out to grass for ever such a long time.

'I thought he must be some sort of silly bugger to risk all the reputation he had built up when he had nothing at all to prove and when there was plenty of good guys around who knew the TT backwards. Not only that, but technically everything had advanced so far since he had last raced bikes. The tyres were stickier now, and compared with those triangulars we used to race on they were light years different. Brakes were better and engines much, much more powerful. The whole scene was altering so radically it was hard enough to keep pace with it when you were still riding, so it seemed to me to be too much to ask a man who had been away so long to adapt to it. Even a man of Hailwood's capability. I thought he was taking far too much of a gamble – and if he hurt himself it would be a disaster for the TT. I was worried that he might fall off. In the event he absolutely astounded me.

'It was my view, before I got to the island, that he would not make a place on the leader board, in the top six. I'm not saying he was discounted as a serious contender, but I just could not see him getting placed. And as for winning, well that was out of the question. What a forecaster I turned out to be!

'After I'd been with him in practice a couple of times and seen how he performed around the old place, I quickly began to change my ideas and come to the conclusion that I was looking at a potential winner. He really was that good. So much so that when a newspaperman came to see me and

Mike

asked me if I thought Phil Read posed a threat, I said "Posed yes, threat no". Hailwood was plainly going to be the man to worry about and pay a lot of attention to in the coming race week.

'I reckon he was a better rider at the TT, after all those years, than he had been during his heyday. He was superb, and he brought a new technique to the place that I hadn't seen before. It must have been the effects of his Formula One car days, because his style was different from anything I'd seen. He was neat, as neat and as tucked-in as ever, but when I saw him practise I thought he had dropped an awful clanger. I was right behind him and I thought on the first corner we came to that he had overshot it. I never saw any other rider go in so deep – he rode on well past the point where I and all the others would peel off, then suddenly flopped the bike over and came across with a vengeance. It was a tremendous sight and he kept on doing it. You might think when you were following that you could get underneath him on the braking and that he had overdone the corner. No chance. When he came back there was no stopping him and no beating him through. It was awesome. And it was safe. I never thought I was going to be cut up and have my road taken; it was his from the moment he threw the bike over and gassed it through what was left of the corner. He seemed to use road that only the sheep walked on, tarmac I'd never been on in all my TTs, and he was going ten miles an hour faster.

'I was fascinated, but then I saw there were two places, Rhencullen and Greeba Bridge, where his line was a world different from mine. Each time I found the smooth bits and he got himself into the bumps by being two yards farther across, but it didn't seem to make any difference at all to his pace. I could see he hadn't lost any of the old TT crafts – ride the bumps, forget the fancy Grand Prix lines and go with the camber even if it means deserting what would be considered to be the perfect racing line. What with that and his ability to brake far later and attack the corners, I was envious.'

From a natural TT record-breaker like Grant, a hero at the Isle of Man where he had won six victories and missed

Above: *Stan Hailwood with Chris Bateman's wife, Betty, and his Rolls-Royce. A self-made millionaire, Stan was a driving force in his son Mike's career.*

Left: *Mike with his sister Chris, Betty Bateman and her son Barry, and Stan's driver – and the ubiquitous Rolls. Mike was 'only a scrawny kid', but the famous Hailwood grin is already there.*

Below: *Mike, aged about 10, ripping up the lawn of his parents' home near Oxford on a cut-down motor-cycle.*

Right: *Competing in the 1957 Scottish Six Days Trial.*

Below: *A classic shot of what are now classic motor-cycles. Hailwood (left), Alan Trow and Dan Shorey, all on Manx Nortons, wait for the off at Aberdare Park in 1959. Mike won 8 out of 9 races that day.*

Above: *Mike's first Grand Prix, the 1959 Dutch TT. He is on a Ducati (4), next to Ernst Degner (MZ, 8) and Tarquinio Provini (2) on an MV.*

Left: *Mike's first ride for MV was at the Italian GP at Monza in 1961, where he won. Here he poses with team manager Nello Pagani (left), Bill Webster (right) and an MV mechanic, Vittorio Carrano.*

Below: *Hailwood (left) and Bill Ivy battling it out on a curling rink. One of the finest riders of his day, Ivy, Phil Read's Yamaha team-mate, was later tragically killed.*

Above: *The famous Honda 250-6, here dwarfed by Hailwood. For its day, the little bike was a miracle of advanced technology, and Mike won many races on it.*

Below: *Phil Read, one of Hailwood's most talented opponents, here seen on a 500cc Norton at the 1963 Dutch TT. 'I was good, but he was better', said Read.*

Left: *After the 'incident' with the police car and the fly-over – Mike leaves court to be greeted by his step-mother, Pat, January 1964.*

Below: *Mike and the Lotus-BRM 25, on their way to sixth place and one Formula One World Championship point at the 1964 Monaco Grand Prix in Monte Carlo.*

Left: *The classic, supremely neat Hailwood style – Mike on the MV in Holland, 1965.*

Left: *Mike and a very battered MV 500 in the 1965 Senior TT in the Isle of Man. Despite having crashed, he remounted and went on to win.*

Below: *Two of the greatest names in road-racing: Hailwood (1) follows his MV team-mate Giacomo Agostini through the wet streets of Sachsenring during the 1965 East German GP. Hailwood went on to win.*

Above: *The evil-handling Honda 500-4, one of the most difficult-to-ride racing motor-cycles ever assembled. Hailwood displays his boot, patched after being nearly worn through by dramatic leaning angles, before the start of the Czechoslovakian GP at Brno in 1966, which he won.*

Left: *Honda team-mates – Jim Redman (left) and Hailwood in 1966. A brilliant rider, Redman was also adept at looking after his fellow riders' rights.*

Hailwood in 1965, before he joined Honda.

Two years later, and the strain of Grand Prix racing is showing in Mike's face: 'Racing has aged me – it's made me an old man before my time', he said.

TT 1978

others through dreadful bad luck, such accolades were praise indeed. I told Mike what Grant had been saying about him.

'You're just trying to gee me up,' he said, 'make me feel better just because things aren't going right. Granty said that? Fantastic. Perhaps the crafty old bugger's seen all my weak points and is just trying to fill me with a sense of security that he'll crack wide open.'

'He must have thought I was a madman,' said Mick, 'when we went round together one night in practice. I trailed him halfway, up to somewhere near Ramsey hairpin, on the way up to the mountain. That was a section where I was absolutely lousy and got lost every time. But I knew Mike was brilliant up there. Anyway, I wanted to follow him over the tops and pick up a few pointers, but he'd had enough of my being behind and at the hairpin he waved me on as if to say "It's your turn." I led him up the mountain and hit all the lines I thought he would be on at racing speeds – and I was all over the place, all wrong just about everywhere, on the grass, off the road and up the bankings. He must have thought I was some sort of crackpot. Either that or a genius who could win, and break the record, and on those crazy lines! My record proved I was a winner at the TT; Mike must have thought I'd done it from a baseline of madness.'

The chase took them both round at a fraction over 113 mph and Grant told me: 'It made my week to keep pace with the great man. I'll never forget it.'

At dinner Mike, going over the evening's business, said: 'How the bloody hell Granty's ever won here I'll never know. I followed him over the mountain and he was all over the place. Frightened the life out of me. He must have been nearly off on every corner, but, Jesus, has he got balls! He's fast all right, but he's got some of the strangest lines you've ever seen.'

When we met a clearly puzzled Tom Herron, the day afterwards, up on the mountain trying to sort out the sequence of the thirty-third milestone, Mike was almost convinced he was racing among lunatics. Herron was riding to-and-fro on a borrowed motor-bike sizing up the approach, the entry and the exit. We were in the Rover, and

Mike

when Mike stopped and wound down the window, the Herron face pushed in and said:

'Give us a clue, Mike, how do you get through this bit so fast?'

But there was no great trick according to Mike. 'I just shut my eyes,' he said. 'That way I don't get scared.'

Mick Grant still feels a great sadness that he never found himself in direct confrontation with Mike; breakdowns, injury and downright bad luck kept them apart in 1978 and 1979 except for a brief, short-lived flurry which counted for nothing.

'That would have been some race,' said Mick, 'if only Mike and I could have gone all the way at the TT. We both had the same determination as never-give-up triers and we could, I'm sure, have really set a cracking pace that might never have been beaten. And if I have one regret from all my racing on the island, it's that Mike and I never got to grips.'

He went on: 'When you think he had not raced the island since 1967, and he had left it with a record lap of more than 108 mph, every bit of it really hard fought, it was amazing that he could get around at the speeds he did. It all just served to show what a true genius he was. There'll never be another like him, that's for sure.'

Phil Read, in Hailwood's day the controversial Yamaha team leader who battled as hard with team-mate Bill Ivy as he did with his rivals – Mike, Jim Redman, Frank Perris, Ernst Degner and Hugh Anderson in the halcyon mid-sixties – had returned to the Isle of Man in 1977 after slamming the place mercilessly. Not only that, but he had registered a marvellous win for Honda in the Formula One class and was the reigning TT champion when Mike was to take him on a year later. He did not know it, but he may have been largely instrumental in sowing the seeds for Mike's reassessment of his racing future on two wheels. Read had told him: 'It's a doddle, and if I can do it you certainly can.' I am convinced that Mike, who had nearly always had the beating of Read in the fiery Grand Prix atmosphere, felt that if it was that easy for Read it would be just as simple for him too.

TT 1978

Read recalls: 'When I heard Mike was going to have another go at the TT, I was really chuffed about it. I felt that his coming back would only do good for the sport in general. There were not too many charismatic characters around and Mike back on the scene would liven it up. I knew he would make my job harder, he was too good a rider, especially at the TT, to have lost his skill and I knew I would have my work cut out whatever he was on. As it turned out, the Ducati was perfectly suited and there was no holding him. He was in tremendous mood and great form and those two features coming together made him unbeatable. I tried as hard as I could – and the bike blew up.'

Mike's respect for Read, even if he did not particularly like him, filled him with a caution that was both wise and necessary. He had always admired Phil's determination and his fearsome single-mindedness and he knew that Phil liked to hold on to what he had won; the TT Formula One title captured the year before would keep Read on a fine edge.

Whatever feelings existed about Mike's comeback *before* practice for the race got under way, they were very quickly altered *afterwards*. His instant competitiveness was seen in the times he logged; eleven years were bridged as if they had never opened up a gap in his motor-cycle race career. Grant and Read were soon aware that Mike's threat on the Ducati was a real one; the Yamahas, the machines to be used for the rest of the week, were rather more of a problem and there seemed to be so little time to sort them out with any guarantee of satisfaction. On the other hand the smaller Ducati back-up, a contrast to the heavy Yamaha presence, hit a good standard almost right away and after a few electrical problems and front suspension difficulties had been ironed out, the Formula One challenge as presented by Hailwood and the 'Duke' began to assume formidable proportions.

A suspension expert who stationed himself on the fearsome Bray Hill, half a mile beyond the start-line, was horrified to see how the big Ducati behaved when Mike hurtled it down the ski-run angle towards its bumpy base. 'It's all over the place,' he said when he returned to the paddock to help in the setting-up. But when he passed his views on to Mike, the great man said: 'Really, that bad, eh? It seemed to be okay to me.'

The suspension man, who had the answer to the problem already worked out in his mind, said: 'Try it this way,' and offered the solution, 'and see if it improves.' And when Mike came back after another practice lap, he could not believe how much it had been improved – but he was quite happy and satisfied to ride it the way it had been. He did not believe it could be improved all that much, so great was his readiness to accept what was given him and make the best of it without causing a fuss.

The Read-versus-Hailwood showdown boiled down to a clash between the Honda's top-end power and the Ducati's better handling, a classic division of advantages, and the intriguing question of whether Mike could take up where he had left off a decade ago with enough verve to master a revitalised Read who was itching to swamp the maestro.

When Read motored into Douglas and called to see Mike at our hotel, he found us relaxing by the swimming pool. Mike in his trunks, sprawled in a deckchair munching his favourite lunch of chicken sandwiches and enjoying a new-found taste for coffee, swapped the usual banter with Read. The cross-talk was about a telegram Read had sent Mike congratulating him on his comeback and remarking 'Hope to see you behind me.' Mike had replied 'Only when I'm lapping you.' It was good-natured stuff, but with deadly serious undertones which added spice to the prospect of another titanic battle between the old enemies. Read's sight of Mike stripped and looking so fit and strong must have gone a long way towards setting back his confidence, for this was no cripple, despite the banana-shaped leg and flat foot, crushed to jelly in the Nürburgring pile-up.

'I knew the look of his backside better than his wife Pauline,' said Read. 'I'd seen it often enough when we were Grand Prix racing. Just another race had become something special with Mike in it and him looking so fit. This was now prestige stuff and I realised that my race the year before had been great for me – but with Mike back I was going to have

TT 1978

to get my finger out and work even harder for the Formula One TT.'

I had arranged Mike's Ducati ride with Steve Wynne's Sports Motorcycles in Manchester, and the tall, bearded Northerner, a sometime racer himself, could not believe his luck. The fee was quickly settled over dinner; it was nothing to do with me how it was mounted, but it was a three-way split between Steve, the London dealers and importers Coburn and Hughes, and the Ducati factory. Wynne was still waiting for the Ducati factory to pay up some years later.

Then, with barely two weeks to go before the bikes were to be shipped to England for the biggest event in the factory's history, the Italian bosses said they could not get insurance for Mike and the Rome headquarters ordered a back-out. Wynne was stunned.

'I couldn't believe it,' said Wynne. 'We were on the brink of the greatest moment in the factory's history and they wanted to drop out. I suppose it was understandable in some ways; after all, who would want to insure Mike against a comeback in the TT? It was, they felt, too much of a risk. The most famous motor-cycle racer of them all racing after an eleven-year interval on the world's toughest circuit. But they were terribly worried, particularly since Peter Williams had sued Norton after his crash at Oulton Park. They didn't want to chance any repeat of that sort of action from a rider – and certainly not one as legendary as Mike. But I knew he wouldn't have sued anybody in a racing accident and I knew everything would be okay. But they wouldn't have it.

'I was faced with only one way out: I had to buy the bikes from the factory – £10,000. And it was a lot of money for me; I was only a small businessman without the big funds the factory had. But they wouldn't even give me any sort of help and I had to pay the bills for the mechanics to come over and assist.

'It wasn't that I begrudged one penny of the whole deal. Sponsors never make any money out of racing; it's the satisfaction you get out of doing something that interests you deeply. And, anyway, the chance to back Mike

Mike

Hailwood would come only once in a lifetime. My main idea was to make sure we did well and stirred the factory's interest so much that it would weigh in with full support the year after. None of this was Mike's business; I didn't want to involve him and have him worry any more than he needed to, so I got on with buying two bikes and making the arrangements for the mechanics.

'The deal was that if Mike won, and there were no accidents, I could sell the bikes back to the factory. The idea of a replica must have been on their minds, and we saw later what a commercial success that became. If he didn't win, then I could keep the machines! At the price I'd paid, of course. They couldn't lose.

'But this was the highlight of my life, the greatest moment of all for me, and I wasn't going to let it slip for the sake of ten grand.

'When I look back on that magical afternoon in June in 1978, I realise it would be impossible to repeat the sensation. Everything afterwards has just been a great anti-climax. How can you follow that? The answer is: you cannot. And my only regret is that it all had to end; but it was a dream come true while it lasted.'

Steve's dreams, in fact, started to turn into stark reality early in practice week when massive crowds, the biggest ever, turned up to watch the rehearsals for the spectacular show. And Mike immediately took up where he had left off – in record-breaking mood. It was quite unbelievable, for in his opening burst he bettered the Formula One lap record set up by Read one year before – 102.69 mph against Phil's fastest of 101.74 mph.

Mike, fourteen pounds lighter and down to his ideal racing weight of eleven stone after all that exercise on his ten-acre home in Auckland, rubbed off all the rust of his dormant years in his very first practice lap. 'I know I could have gone a lot quicker,' he told me, 'but I could hardly see. There were flies plastered all over my visor. But I'm happy the way it all fitted together; I had no real problems remembering where I was going or where I should be on the road.'

TT 1978

He followed it up with his first blast on the 500cc Yamaha – and was clocked at 105.70 mph, the fastest of the session. The impossible, it seemed, was turning into a real probability – and even Mike was starting to believe in fairy tales.

A couple of nights later he touched an absolute personal best at the TT, 111.04 mph, marginally short of Mick Grant's course record of 112.77 mph set up on the 750cc Kawasaki in 1977. It was the night before the curtain-raising Formula One race, his comeback clash. And there could not have been a more appropriate time to get his rivals looking to their own best and worrying about this man from the past, this bald thirty-eight-year-old, still sniffing and short of breath from a heavy cold, and limping onto the grid with his gammy leg in the hope of wiping out the passing years.

He hoped, but was still not sure, that he could do the job. 'It's really too much to ask,' he said, as he tried to take all the vivid expectancy out of the situation. 'What perks me up,' he went on, 'is that when I did 111 it felt nowhere like that sort of speed. It was easy, very easy, and I didn't come anywhere near frightening myself. Not once. I can't believe it was that fast. It's as if I was never away from the island; all the tricky bits I can remember were exactly where I expected them to be and nothing took me by surprise. I'm not saying I'm going to win – but I'll certainly give Phil Read a bloody good run for all the money they're paying him.' And he went to bed with a sleeping tablet.

The statistics of success, piled up behind him, seemed to point towards victory. Having seen him at close range for nearly two weeks, even before practice, and watched the steadfastness of his preparation, seen the look in his eyes and fastened onto unwittingly offered hints about his chances, I believed quite firmly that the Formula One winner was asleep in room 333.

I wrote in my newspaper, the *Daily Mirror*, on the morning of the race: 'I am as certain as I can be that he will win this, the first race of the week – but only after a tremendous battle with Read's Honda, a machine that may not make it to the finish.' I added: 'In hard terms he will push Formula One title-holder Phil Read to the very limits of

Mike

his Honda's stamina, maybe even to engine-breaking point.' How prophetic!

Certainly Read, unhappy with Honda and having a torrid time with the Japanese team's set-up, was far from content with the way the machine was going to carry him in this dire challenge to its island supremacy. Meanwhile, Mike set himself the plan of lapping at around 106 mph, to play a waiting game on the record-breaking pace, and see what developed in the Honda scheme of things.

The outcome, as we all know, was one of memorable triumph for Mike, and even in the widest reaches of sport of any kind, anywhere in the world, there can hardly have been a more dramatic, more stirring comeback. To share it was to live to the heights. And there were more than enough tears of emotion shed openly by grown men, hardened by years of racing, tears which said all that was needed to be said about feelings, affection and pride at being involved. I was among them. So was Steve Wynne. And Mike too cried streams. It was, quite simply, the most marvellous moment at the point of victory that any one of us had ever felt. Who could ever forget it? Who among those thousands of spectators dared deny that he had just witnessed an event that would be frozen in the mind's eye for as long as they lived?

In the time-elapse which is used at the TT, Mike gave Phil Read fifty seconds' start and then, as remorselessly and as surely as tomorrow follows today, he stole all the time back and hacked away at Read's fine reputation as one of the great riders of the age; Mike was proving himself, as he had done so often before, to be even greater. The genius was in full flow and neither Read at his best and his fastest, nor anybody else on that day, could have resisted the charge that was firing Mike's determination and sending him headlong into racing's memory. Mike's skill may have been deep-frozen for a few years, but when he cracked it open, there it was in pristine form, as good as new.

His race plan was coolly precise. He had mentally computed the best chances of the opposition and programmed that against what he knew they had left after he had frightened everybody off with that confidence-killing

TT 1978

practice lap of 111 mph. After that, it was simple. All he had to do was give full rein to his natural flair. A lap in temper had taken Read around at 109-plus, but it had surprised even him and we knew he could not better it in the race. Neither, Mike reasoned, could Herron or John Williams go much quicker, even if they had wanted to, in a bid to cancel out the Ducati.

Once Mike had caught and passed Read's Honda and Phil had sent it cripplingly into the red-line zone, it was necessary only to keep watch on John Williams's progress and hold station on the distance he had built up between them. Read's challenge ended in a splutter after eleven miles of the last lap but one. Herron's Honda too, having closed to within four seconds, faded out of the picture. It left John Williams struggling as manfully as ever, two minutes in arrears in second place, and Ian Richards, four minutes behind Mike, in third place. At the end Mike had established a new lap record of 110.27 mph and had completed the 226-mile race at a new record average of 109.51, the distance covered in 2 hours 5 minutes 10.2 seconds. Those eleven long years had evaporated into nothing.

'Right from the off people were cheering me. On every corner there were hundreds waving programmes and handkerchiefs,' said Mike. 'It was fantastic. On the slow bits, like the hairpin at Ramsey or through Parliament Square, I could hear them. It wasn't half a spur! I'd never seen that before, not in all the years I'd done at the TT.

'And then to go on and win ... well ... honestly ... I have never felt anything like it in my whole life. It was indescribable. All the feelings I had kept bottled up just burst out and – I'm not ashamed to admit it – I cried like a baby when I was heading for the chequered flag. My eyes were so filled up I could barely see the line. It was the most emotional moment I've ever known, greater than any world title I'd won, stronger than any race I have ever been in. It will stay with me as my fondest memory in racing until the day I die.'

The celebration party that night was a riot and Mike broke his teetotal fast in a mad, mad spree that had the local

Mike

police turning a blind eye and, much later, near dawn, a dozen or so new hotel guests wondering what had made their toilets flush on their own in the night. But it was no mystery to me how a six-foot potted palm got into my bed or why, when I woke up, I did not have one pair of trousers on any of the hangers in my wardrobe.

Over a late breakfast, when the adrenalin was still pumping in Mike's veins, he talked me through the duel in the sun of the afternoon before. The magnificent reality of it all was not distanced in any way by the passing hours, much as they had been filled with wild goings-on. And Mike obviously found great fulfilment in going over the events, as if it would somehow salve the surprise he was still registering at the wonder of it all.

'I was so filled up by the crowd's reaction to what I was trying to do,' he said, 'that it was hard to concentrate. But I knew I had to; it was vital to ignore as much as I could what was going on all around the course. I had to get on with the job and I'm sure people would realise that.

'I had been concentrating like mad, worrying that the lead I had built up from the beginning might all be lost if I did something silly. So much so that I lost count of the laps and at the end I still wasn't sure if there was another one to go. Then I saw the flag, of course. Usually people don't wave quite as wildly until the end, until the very last lap, but they had been doing it all the way from the start and I suppose it fooled me.

'What gave me a big kick was catching up with Ready. I'd given him fifty seconds and when I saw him up ahead of me I thought it was somebody else and I was trying to do my sums in my head to work out if it could really be him and the Honda. He certainly wasn't looking round for anybody; he was down to the business of trying to keep that wobbly old Honda on a straight course. When I drew level he got a bit of a shock. I could see that by his face, the way he looked across at me. We played about for a while, had a bit of tomfoolery between us with him flapping his elbows out as I went past him on the approach to Ramsey.

'But Phil being Phil, he had to put on a bit of a show of

TT 1978

resistance and as we headed into Parliament Square he outbraked me where the crowd was at its biggest and gave me a V-sign over his shoulder. I let him get on with it and followed him through. He was entitled to his bit of fun. We had a bit of a dice for a while, then I got a signal that Tom Herron was really on his way, so I decided to clear off and leave Phil to his own devices; there was no point in hanging around with him. But then poor old Tom, who had been riding really well and who was flying, ran into trouble and dropped out of the running. After that, I was pretty much on my own; I knew John Williams was a long way back and Ian Richards even farther.

'It all turned out to be relatively easy. Phil's Honda burned itself out in the effort and I ran home an easy winner, much easier than I had thought it was going to be when I was sitting on the start-line. Truthfully, I was well within my safety limits, seven-tenths, well below 100 per cent effort, and with plenty left in hand had I needed it. There's no doubt at all I could have gone a good deal quicker had it been necessary, but it was never a question of having to stick my neck out. And once I had caught and passed Phil, my main threat, I knew the race was as good as won. It was then down to a matter of prayer that the Ducati would hang together, but I hadn't stressed it at all and there was not much danger of it breaking. Steve Wynne had done a sterling job on the preparation – I couldn't have asked for more. It was fast enough and far more stable than the Honda Read was on; that one took my mind back to the last ride I had had at the TT, in 1967 when that pig of a 500 tried to throw me off just about every yard of the way. I'd had my fill of Hondas and I knew what Phil was feeling. Mine was an easy chair of a ride.

'I kept it below 7,500 revs on the last lap and nursed it like a baby all the way home. The scenes at the grandstand were unforgettable and I don't mind admitting I was blinking back the tears.'

Read, still in his leathers, called to see Mike after the race to offer his congratulations. Later he told me: 'What else could I do? The man's just incredible. I never thought he'd

Mike

beat me, but we were thrashed out of sight. I just had to drive round to the hotel to see him and tell him.'

What followed Hailwood's historic triumph was Yamaha's shame. Quite frankly, they were a sad let-down for the rest of the week and Martini, who had happily tied up with the Grand Prix élite for what they hoped would be a TT bonanza, must have felt somebody had let the air out of their high-flying balloon, though they were far too dignified an organisation to admit it, or to level blame. It seemed to me, having arranged for Mike to be backed by Yamaha in the break they had between world championship chasing, that Yamaha made only a half-hearted bid in the belief that Mike could not possibly justify any more effort after such a long lay-off. Many of their errors were elementary and contrasted cruelly with the painstaking, deep-seated effort and sheer sweat and all-night toil gruellingly undertaken by Wynne and his tiny team in the Sports Motorcycles set-up. Maybe Yamaha thought their reputation was enough to frighten off the others; Ducati and Wynne harboured no such misguided views and made sure, doubly sure, that Mike had a machine that would be fully capable of matching any ambitions he had for it. The Yamaha operation spluttered and banged along with none of the ritual smoothness it had enjoyed on the Grand Prix front; perhaps the absence of Kel Carruthers, the wizard team leader in the championships, made all the difference.

Mike's racing friend Dickie Attwood, a close confidant, put it all in perspective when he said: 'Yamaha were a bloody disgrace and a big let-down. Had they done their bit as well as Sports Motorcycles had done theirs, Mike might have had a clean sweep at the TT. He would most certainly have won at least one more race. They were guilty in my mind of absolutely shameful treatment of the whole business. They failed to understand the seriousness of it all, let him down badly, and worst of all wasted a wonderful talent when they could, if they had thought about it for longer than a minute or two, have wrapped up the TT almost all to themselves. Instead they threw it all away when it was right there in their hands. Mike would have won again that

TT 1978

week if only the Yamaha people had given him half a chance. As it was, they blundered badly.'

Mike never publicly voiced his utter disappointment at the way the rest of the week progressed – or rather did *not* progress – though it was plain to his close circle of friends that he was far from happy that his back-up had fallen well short of his requirements. With a substantial array of international sponsors lined up behind him and the eyes of the entire racing world focused in his direction, he just could not curb the old feelings of responsibility that had always weighed heavily on his mind; he had always striven to give a fair deal and maximum effort in return for whatever support, financial or otherwise, he ever received throughout his entire career. And not even at the height of his racing exploits had he been backed with such wide-ranging and massive sponsorship. Indeed, he had always shunned it in the past, saying he could not be bothered and he was earning enough money to keep him happy. The upshot was that he limited his support to the sport's identifiable backers; the oil and petrol companies, race wear and, for a while, a cigarette company, even though he never smoked. Money was never a prime concern in Mike's career. I suppose it could be argued that, since he already had plenty, he could afford to have that view – but that would be to misunderstand his whole attitude to life and racing. He had lost plenty of opportunities to make a bigger pile – by doing people favours, by accepting readily what they offered even though both he and they knew it was money well short of what realistically he should have been paid. The TT in 1978 was a different case; he was contented with what his worth was reckoned to be commercially, and he knew that he could make money with his own effort and skill. If the machines stood up to the job in hand ...

But one after the other the 500, the 250 and the 750 Yamahas let him down. A steering-damper on the 500 broke in the Senior, the race he had almost made his own in the past with five wins. He was third at the time, but the work which had to be done in the pits pushed him right out of the running.

Mike

Despite the set-backs he kept on going and finished twenty-eighth – nobody would have blamed him if he had pulled out and slipped away from the inevitable crush of attention to the comparative haven of our hotel, but quitting was never part of his nature. There was something else for him to go for and it kept him out there in the fray, down among the also-rans; his quickest ever TT lap. And he managed it on lap five – a speed of more than 112 mph, comparing favourably with Pat Hennen's record lap of 113·83 mph. 'At least I got something out of it', he said, 'and I know I could have been up there with the leaders if the thing had stayed in once piece.' Tom Herron won after Pat Hennen had crashed mysteriously at about 165 mph when he was chasing hard, too hard maybe, for victory on his Suzuki. He has never raced again.

Monday's Senior gloom gave way to Wednesday's Lightweight disappointment, though Mike had never fancied his chances on the little 250, as nice a bike as it was. He had managed only two practice laps on it and had fallen off at Braddan Bridge, and he knew there were so many hard-going 250cc specialists in the running that it was going to be an impossible task. The only useful purpose it could serve was as extra practice for the big show, Friday's Classic confrontation with Mick Grant. Another blunder, however, served to wreck Mike's chances of getting a good result when, inevitably, he got the taste for action once the race was in full flow. The fuel tank was too small and he had to make one stop more than the other runners and finished in twelfth place. Then a broken crankshaft snapped his chances of victory over Grant's Kawasaki in the £10,000 Classic and left 400 pressmen and thousands of fans on the island pondering what might have been but for the big Yamaha's first-lap fade-out.

Mike's disappointment was immense. He blamed himself for letting down so many people, and none of it was cancelled out in his view by the memorable Formula One comeback win on Saturday afternoon. That, to him, was history. What counted, he said, was that so many people had gone to so much trouble to travel to the Isle of Man to see

TT 1978

him on Friday and he had done nothing to justify their expensive trip to give them anything to talk about on the way home.

The wear and tear on him mentally and physically, not only from the racing – and that was hard enough – but from the surrounding attentions of fans and media alike, had forced all the bounce out of him by the end of what had been a momentous fortnight. He had headaches, was desperately tired and his wrists, bandaged for racing, were aching and racked with the effort of using the clutch and front brake – he rarely used the back – and with holding the throttle hard against the springs. But he was prepared to go through it all again, not for his own sake, but for those disappointed fans who were not disappointed at all. Mike, I felt, had misread their feelings, but had pumped in his own and was inconsolable on the matter. He staggered me by saying, even before we left the island: 'Let's do it again next year.' I could not believe my ears. And off he went to Mallory Park on the totally unsuitable Ducati to take on the hardened 'scratchers' around the Midlands oval. And what a huge crowd followed him. They certainly had their money's worth, for Mike won again, and in such style and with such fiery determination after an awful start which left him deep down the field, that there seemed to be no end to the fairy tale.

Steve Wynne, who had fettled the Ducati into good order after the TT, though it had survived the Formula One effort without any problems at all, wheeled out the new world-title winner at Mallory without much hope that Mike could repeat the success.

'But it was incredible, he did it all over again. And in many ways it was a better performance than the TT,' he said later, 'and he did it without a back brake. Only the front was working, but he didn't care. Many other riders would have packed it in, skating around Mallory with only the front stopper operating, but not Mike. He wasn't even sure how many gears the bike had and he asked me before the race if it had six – and he'd done hundreds of miles in practice and racing in the Isle of Man!

'I watched him closely at Mallory and he was fantastic; he

was on lines nobody else ventured anywhere near, and they were perfect.

'He went very, very deep into the corners, way beyond them almost, then threw the bike over, scrubbed off the speed, and cut out any chances anybody had of getting under him. He was brilliant. It was vintage Hailwood and he set the crowd alight. It was twenty laps of genius, of *pure* genius, with Mike fighting from way down until he hit the front, then holding it and running away almost unchallenged.'

'Breathtaking stuff all right,' said Mick Grant. 'It was a performance that went all the way to showing just what made the man so great. But it was impossible to copy his racing lines – only he seemed to have the balance to use them. They were totally different from anybody else's, but they were most certainly effective. And you've got to remember one thing: all those other guys out there were regular, week-in week-out racers and most of them knew Mallory Park as a regular stamping ground. Mike hadn't even seen the place for about ten years or more. It made his win all the more remarkable. When you watch the video of the race, you can see his determination was really locked on to a win. Nothing else was in his mind and the way he picked off those chaps ahead of him after getting such a dreadful start was an awesome sight. We'll never see his like again.'

Wynne, by now an unashamed worshipper of the Hailwood genius, told me afterwards: 'Looking back you just don't realise how good he really was, not until you deal with other riders. Not that they're bad, or slow, it's just that he was head and shoulders above the best there was. I have to keep on reminding myself that when he raced my Ducati he was thirty-eight, in against all the eager youngsters and regular racers, and he was doing it with a leg and a foot that were in a hell of a mess. But he was *still* better than anybody else, with all their bits and pieces in good order and even with quicker machinery.'

4

TT 1979

A year later we were back on the TT trail – but what a difference there was this time. Ducati, no doubt embarrassed that Wynne had done it almost all alone in 1978, moved experts in to help him and his partner Pat Slinn, one of the quieter forces behind Mike's success. But it was a backwards step, and while Mike's instructions for the 1979 TT were simply to put on a bigger rear wheel and beef up the power a bit, they overdid the development and tried to redesign what was already a proven winner to such a degree that the 'improvements' proved counter-productive. The Ducati was 20 bhp more powerful – and 10 mph slower. The handling, so beautifully behaved the year before, became wayward and left Mike bitter that their interference had set his chances back just as surely as if they had planned it. Ducati could not have been more reckless or thoughtless and Steve Wynne, even more disappointed at their back-up in 1979 than he had been when they had stayed out in 1978, was furious. He still is.

'We thought we'd have a superb factory machine, instead they sent us a pile of crap,' he said, 'and I'll never forgive them as long as I live. They let me and Mike down at a time when they'd had a year to get things dead right. It was a

Mike

fiasco – the gearboxes were useless and the frame was no good at all. We had to strive really hard to make enough modifications to give Mike some semblance of a chance, but we were fighting a losing battle. It was a slovenly effort from the factory and I had to put more money in to try and salvage something.

'But nobody should get the idea I'm moaning about it. It cost me something like £30,000 over the two TTs I backed Mike, but I still consider it the best investment I ever made. I don't regret one penny I spent. I'd do it again tomorrow if I could. And double it, if I thought I could do it all over with Hailwood.'

Attwood, too, was furious and he said: 'They threw it away. They wouldn't listen to Mike. They blindly went on what they thought was an improvement schedule and it just set the bike back. When they finished, it was far worse than the one Mike had won on in 1978. What the bloody hell were they playing at? They didn't need the best bike, they already had the best rider. But their stupid thinking reasoned it all out quite wrongly and instead of giving Mike the best chance, they left him with none at all.'

Mike's view was: 'I'm sure they didn't intend to build a bad bike, but what they have given me is one that comes nowhere near the excellence of last year's. A bit more power and a bigger back wheel and I know I could have done an adequate job. I'm just sorry for Steve Wynne and the lads. They've had to work like demons trying to get it right. But it's too late, really, to do anything. I'll give it a go, but I know I'm fighting a losing battle unless we get a huge stroke of luck.'

The factory mechanics had even managed to put the gear lever on the wrong way round, and when Mike went to Italy for a test session at Misano he changed down instead of up at about 130 mph on a long bend, and was pitched over the bars. He was lucky not to be killed, but he cracked a couple of ribs and there was barely a month to go before the TT. He flew home, helped by Champion plugs fitter Vince French, in terrible pain, and when he phoned me to tell me the extent of his injuries he was extremely depressed. Shortly afterwards

TT 1979

Tom Herron, the irrepressible Irishman who had become such a firm friend, was killed racing at Ulster's terrifyingly fast North-West 200, and his death took Mike right to the brink of quitting. It was only his sense of loyalty to those who were supporting him that eased him through the big black void that had opened up underneath him. On top of all these setbacks he was struggling to set up a business in Birmingham, trying to sell a virtually unsaleable house that had been threatened by a landslide in New Zealand, and set up a new home somewhere in the Midlands, close to his new motor-cycle dealership in which he was partnered by Rod Gould, the former world 250cc champion and Yamaha executive.

'It's all starting to get me down,' he told me. 'Tom's death, the crash in Italy – and that's still hurting like mad – and all this business of getting settled in England again. As if I haven't enough on my mind, I don't think the Ducati is up to the job. It's miles slower and doesn't handle at all well. Maybe when I get to the island I can put all these difficulties behind me and get stuck into concentrating on the racing.'

He went on ahead of me. When I arrived a day later, he met me at Ronaldsway Airport, disguised in dark glasses, baseball cap peak pulled right down over his face, and pressed into a corner by a pillar where nobody would see him. But his mood had changed dramatically: he was a much happier, more contented, more relaxed Mike. If there had been anything to lift him, it was Suzuki's style in the long run-up to the TT. I had contacted Suzuki-GB and invited them to support Mike with a 500 in the Senior and the Classic, and they could not have been happier. Now they were on the island and their expertise was filling him with confidence again. They *looked* and *were* a superbly professional team and none of the confusion that had seemed to reign in the Yamaha back-up the year before invaded their work.

The test sessions and Mike's first try-out of the Suzuki had gone like a dream; nobody could understand that while Grand Prix stars in the team made endlessly fussy changes in between each practice session, Mike, despite warnings about

Mike

the bike's vagaries, could find little or nothing wrong or to alter. He was content. And the mood he had enjoyed with Suzuki in mainland testing had followed him to the island for the real business. Race headquarters at the Majestic Hotel overlooking Douglas was a cheerful place to be on any day; pride shone as brightly as any engine part and the urgency of it all rubbed off on Mike. He loved it, he was starting to tingle and could not wait to get to grips with his love-hate TT course.

His confidence had taken a marvellous upturn even by the time a recorded television interview was going out in which he said: 'I don't feel so enthusiastic this year. I have a lot of personal pressures building up, a lot of things on my mind, and I have not had time to get tuned in to the idea of riding again. I'm finding it very difficult – and I'm still suffering a bit in the rib department after my tumble in Italy. I just hope the people out there don't expect too much. I'll do my best and that's the only promise I can make.'

He had plenty of moral support. Friends were flying in again from all over the world and this year I had made sure the off-track pressures were not as intense as they had been in 1978. I had rented a house for him and he split his time between there, where he could play the piano and a borrowed guitar to his heart's content, and the Palace-Casino Hotel where he could enjoy teetotal fun with his friends.

And he told me: 'I don't stand a snowball in hell's chance of winning the Formula One – the Senior's a different matter. That should be okay. All I have to do is get through Saturday's job without falling off that Ducati. It's a pig.

'And if anybody thinks I'm spoofing, they should have been sitting where I was when Alex George went by me on the Honda. I was having a distinctly uncomfortable time manhandling the thing through Union Mills when Alex overtook me – he went away like a shot out of a gun. In no time he was gone, out of sight. And it was no surprise to me that he had lapped at 112 and beaten the record I'd set up last year. Jesus, that Honda's quick! I've no chance the way things are, not unless he blows up.

'My bike gets into such frightening wobbles, all over the

TT 1979

place, straights and flats as well as bends and long curves, it's scaring the pants off me. I thought I was being a bit too fussy, but my old mates Eddie Roberts and George Fogarty confirm all my fears. It's happening to them too. It reminds me of that old Honda 500 I used to battle with; it's got that hinged-in-the-middle feel to it. I don't think I'll be able to get round even as fast as I did when I won in '78. It's such a headache and we've beaten our brains to find the solution. But, I'm afraid, it's no-go ...'

Wynne even sent away for the 1978 machine and spent the night before the race working to piece together a decent bike from the others he had lined up. Neither Fogarty nor Eddie Roberts minded in the least, for they knew the team's best shot for the title lay in Mike's hands if only Steve could get the Ducati to behave itself. It was an impossible task and Wynne, despite his and Slinn's efforts, was defeated. Not that Mike did not give it a tremendously brave effort, one that had Pat Slinn purring: 'Probably one of his really great rides at the TT when you consider the state the bike was in and how dangerous it must have felt.' There was an even greater one to come later on in the week, and it too left him without a win. But there was to be glory in defeat for Mike in his last TT – and one final flourish for the record books.

But first, the Formula One. It went precisely as Mike had both feared and expected. The moneybags Honda team, watched by high-ranking Japanese chiefs, threw contract-seeking Alex George, a Scotsman later Isle of Man-based, into the front line with their works 997cc four. Alex wanted a win to earn enough recognition to be signed up; Honda desperately wanted to avenge the humiliation Mike and the Ducati had forced on them in pinching their world title a year ago, when their mighty factory was overshadowed by Steve Wynne's shop-standard Ducati pepped up with a few special bits he had gathered in from California.

Grant should have been aboard the George Honda, but he was injured and the determined Scot, who had dieted victoriously well to reduce his burly frame, was given the responsibility of riding out the Hailwood threat. He may have thought Mike was playing a game of fool-you with his

Mike

practice times, but he was in no mood to hang around to find out. A works ride was up for grabs for him and to beat Hailwood for the first time on such a stage was his main problem.

There could hardly have been a yard of trackside space that was not filled by some eager race fan; the ferries and the planes had shuttled and streamed thousands into the island. Hotel rooms were at a premium, restaurant tables impossible to get, chip-shop queues hundreds of yards long and the pubs, when there was no racing, jammed to the door. It was boom time on what had become the Isle of Mike.

And when we drove up to the grandstand before the start of the Formula One race, the promenade was totally deserted, whereas only an hour or so beforehand it had been thronged with excited fans. In this atmosphere it would have been impossible not to feel a sense of urgency to spice up the adrenalin-flow and Mike's determination to do as well as he could grew larger as the start drew nearer. If it could be done by the man, it would be done – but the machine, unfortunately, was the ultimate factor and it sabotaged whatever lingering hope Mike had.

Ron Haslam, a kid from Nottinghamshire who had curbed his worrying wildness and was a definite goer at the TT, had the second of the works Hondas and Cheshireman Charlie Williams, an island expert with a bundle of wins behind him, was turned loose on David Dixon's Maxton-framed Honda. Up front, Alex George's red, white and blue machine throbbed with a vitality that was clearly missing from the Ducati, four places behind at the start. Mike, chasing hard, held fourth place and even edged Haslam's works bike into his wake when he moved into third spot at the halfway mark in the 226-mile race. But it was a fight and, as he had forecast before the off, he could not even match the pace he had set so easily, so effortlessly, the year before.

He swept past the pits at the start of the last lap, the sixth, and plunged down Bray Hill wishing it was all over and done with, worn out with the effort of fighting for every inch of advantage he had built up over his chasers, but not able to get any closer to the leaders, the Honda pair George and

TT 1979

Williams.

Then, as if he did not have enough trouble to cope with, the top gear went. And with only four out of five working he could not hold off Haslam who repassed him into third place. The Ducati was overrevving sickeningly and suddenly the motor cut out – the vibration had shattered the welding which held the battery bracket, so that the battery worked loose and fell off – only the wires were holding it on. Mike stopped at Hillberry, about two miles from the finish, and reconnected the leads – it was a miracle he knew what to do! – then had to push-start *up hill* to fire the bike up again. It was a credit to his strength and fitness that he could do it, but by the time he had got back into what had become a faltering stride, the young newcomer Graeme Crosby, the New Zealander, had passed him, relegating Mike to fifth place.

'What a race,' he said afterwards. 'I'm absolutely wrecked. I was whacked as it was without having to push the bike up Hillberry. I never realised how steep it is just there until I started to try and fire the bike. Everything went wrong. The handling was as bad as we feared and it gave me a scary old ride. I could not go anywhere near as quick as last year. Top gear went. The battery fell off. And halfway through the race the exhaust pipes fell to bits. All in all a most unsatisfactory situation which I would not care to live through again. No thanks.' And back came the big grin – he knew he had the Senior to come. The Suzuki, he knew, was in pristine condition ... or was it?

Neither team manager Rex White nor chief mechanic Martin Ogborne, a Hailwood fan all his life, could get over Mike's attitude and readiness to ride what he was given without demur or complaint. They had been living with the fickleness of Barry Sheene and the other fussy Suzuki works riders, who never seemed to be satisfied with other machines, whatever work went into them and however late the mechanics had to labour to get them the way they wanted.

For men who had lived on a knife-edge of restraint in the face of the heavy demands of the bloated Grand Prix stars and their enormous self-esteem, Mike's easy-going nature

Mike

took some getting used to. Rex White, a seasoned campaigner in racing at all levels, was one man who enjoyed the reduction in the tempo when he came into Mike's orbit, and he admitted:

'We honestly couldn't believe it when Mike came in after his first practice. Here we go, we thought. This is where our work starts. And he said to Martin Ogborne, "That's okay, no problems at all. It feels really good and it'll do nicely for me."

'We'd had only a handful of fitting and testing sessions before the island and we could not believe we had got it right first time. After all the experiences we'd had with Barry and the others, we expected a whole range of changes to be wanted by Mike. Martin wondered what had hit him. He didn't know what to do. So he kept Mike talking for about an hour just to make sure he really felt it was all okay. In the end Mike gave him one or two minor changes to make, the bars down a bit and the gear lever a bit longer, something and nothing, but I'm sure only suggested by Mike to give Martin and his guys something to do. The bike was as near standard as you could get and, it seemed, we'd made all the right settings for it. We had three different types of fuel tank, for instance; some narrow, some wide, something for every build of rider, really. And the one we'd put on for Mike was just right. At least he said it was. The footpegs and the seat stayed standard and he said he was happy and comfortable. And, really, the whole bike looked lovely. We'd had it painted red, white and gold – Mike's own famous colours – and it was a treat to look at. Martin had set it up from all his past experience at the TT and he seemed to have got it spot-on first time out. There seemed to be hardly anything to do except strip it and clean the bits and keep the bike polished.

'Martin, who thought Mike was some sort of God, spent the whole time in a high state of excitement; after a long career in racing he was looking after the great man. It was something he never imagined he would ever be in a position to do.

'Morale was running very high because of Mike's

TT 1979

presence; the whole outfit was in a buzz, not only on the island but back at the workshops in London. And we were all determined not to let him down – there was going to be no repeat of the 1978 Yamaha débâcle. We knew Mike was going to race sensibly, he realised he had the perfect machine for the task in the Senior and he wouldn't have to be taking any unnecessary risk. We were all very apprehensive about him getting hurt on our bike, of course, but we felt the pairing was right. He had made up his mind that he could win and do it without stretching himself, he had that much confidence in the bike.

'I have to admit we had been disappointed the year before when he rode for Yamaha. I would have loved him to have ridden our bikes, and ages before, a long time before he had even thought about making a comeback, I'd told him that if ever he wanted a good machine, he should get in touch with me. When he went to Yamaha, I thought he didn't love us any more – so when you asked us for a bike I was flabbergasted. But what a marvellous boost for us.

'Martin couldn't contain himself. He had always rated Mike the world's number one of all time and he was almost mesmerised by the magic of it all. We put no pressure on Mike at all – I didn't say I expected him to win, for though it would be nice and rewarding, the opposition in our two races was going to be very stiff. But, after all, he was the greatest, he had won easily the year before, so why shouldn't he do it again? My only reservations were that he was not really a two-stroke rider, but he took to it like a duck to water, just as if he'd never ridden anything else. But that was the measure of the man's greatness, something some people had lost sight of – he could ride any machine you cared to wheel out for him.

'If there was any pressure at all, it was on us, the team. The guys who had to get the bike in race-winning condition for him. We all shared the feeling that it would be a sin to let him down and that we could afford to make no mistakes in the preparation. It just had to be perfect. We were all pepped up in that respect – nothing was going to be left to chance, not with Suzuki.'

Mike

The 500, standing in the lock-up garage at the Majestic Hotel, had not been touched since Mike's final practice run on Friday night. It was Sunday, the day before the Senior. Martin said: 'I'll just give it a run-up.' The bike crackled into life and started pouring smoke out of one pipe; no amount of throttle blip could clear it and it was pretty evident, even to the unpractised eye among the curious bystanders, that something was seriously wrong.

There was a fault on an oil-seal spring and oil, filtering through over the weekend, had filled the crankcase. 'It was just a fluke, really, that we found it,' said Rex White, 'and we had to work right through the night to put it right. Martin and the other fellows got no sleep at all – and they were up at the grandstand at 5 am getting the petrol fillers in place. What it left us with, of course, was an unknown quantity. We could not in any way guarantee how the machine would be after it had been rebuilt. It had been in perfect nick but for that spring. If it had happened on the line, we wouldn't have stood an earthly, but the gods were on our side and we were able to fix it. Or so we hoped. We were certainly a lot less confident than Mike had given us cause to be with his practice performances. But there was nothing else we could do. In the event Martin and his team did a fine job.'

Whatever doubts Mike may have secretly nursed, it made no difference at all to his endeavours; from the off he was set to make it his day after the Formula One wipe-out. His first-lap caution was a sensible approach, he wanted to make sure the machine was capable of responding fully to the task he was about to force it to undertake.

Mick Grant, a near-cripple from a crash that had left him needing to be assisted onto his bike, set a brave dash despite a pelvic crack that made his eyes water with pain every bump of the way. He charged into a first-lap lead ahead of Alex George with Mike patiently feeling out the Suzuki and anxious not to be dropped off the pace.

The Glaswegian, George, was all fired up after his Formula One triumph; Grant, as gritty as he was, knew inside that he could not possible last out six gruelling laps of intense buffeting – but he was spared reluctant retirement

TT 1979

when the Suzuki's crankshaft broke, dropped him back into third place, then finally put him out of the race on lap three, after nearly 113 miles of agony and courageous effort. The man was willing enough, but the machine's steel heart gave way.

Mike reversed a 2.6-second deficit on George and threaded his way in front by the same margin on lap two – but he had to notch up his first sub-20-minute lap at the TT. He stretched it to 8.8 seconds on lap three, drumming up a new record to beat Pat Hennen's best with a lap of 19 minutes 51.2 seconds and flying clear of his chasers. Alex George ran into trouble and lost nearly one minute as he started lap five, but then he too had to abandon his pursuit and left Tony Rutter, one of the real quick men on the island, and Dennis Ireland, a New Zealander of immense road-racing skills, to try and break what was becoming Mike's unshakeable stranglehold on the Senior trophy. But once Mike's Saturday tormentor, George, had been forced onto the sidelines, it was all over bar the considerable shouting which greeted a Hailwood victory at a new record. He was more than two minutes ahead of the Birmingham veteran Rutter's Suzuki at the flag, with Ireland just about half a minute adrift of him in third place. Mike had gone round at 114.02 mph for his stunning new lap record and had completed the 226 miles in 2 hours 1 minute 32.4 seconds, another record. At the end of the week George was to earn his revenge and Mike was to cover the same distance 22 seconds quicker, but still not quick enough to beat an inspired Scotsman riding the race of his life. An epic Classic of unforgettable majesty.

The Senior, the old blue riband race, was the one Mike most wanted to clinch. It was his fourteenth, and last, TT victory, a nostalgic touch of magic to a glittering career which was ending in dazzling style.

After the Senior, when Mike and I were up at the house, out of reach of the clamour of well-wishers and getting ready for a welcome break with a night on the town, he said: 'I'd love to quit right now, while I'm ahead. To finish on this high note. I can't better it. I might match it, but that's all and

Mike

I wish with all my heart my TT career was over and done with tonight. It was wonderful this afternoon, almost as emotional as last year when I won the Formula One, and I couldn't help waving both my fists in the air when I crossed the line. I was as happy as a dog with two tails.

'I suppose I was so fired up after Saturday's flop that I felt I owed it to everybody to do well today. I felt on top form, real good – you know, when you *know* you can do *anything* and *nobody* can shake you. That good. Really, *that* good.

'But I had problems too. Plenty of them. I was set on being patient, making sure I didn't do anything silly and not be panicked into a mistake if anybody cracked off to a good pace. I held myself in check. There was no way I was going to overreach myself whatever anybody else did. I was confident that the Suzuki was okay; it felt fine. It was just a matter of me keeping myself in harness and in the final analysis it all went exactly as I had planned. It didn't matter to me how much pressure anybody tried to put on me early on, I was dead set in my own mind what sort of pace I was going to be happy at, and it didn't surprise me at all that Mick Grant went so well. I always felt I was the man in charge of things and I had to try nowhere near as hard as I did in the Formula One race; if the need had arisen, I know I could have lifted the lap record to more than 115 miles an hour, that's how relaxed I was. Once I had got over Mick's charge and worked out what I had to do if he maintained it, I could take things relatively easy.

'The troubles I had started on the third lap. I had a steering problem and it was difficult to get the bike round slow right-hand corners; luckily there weren't too many of them, but I had to put my foot down to dab my way round what there were and it was a bit dodgy.

'And just when I had got myself into a comfortable lead with only one lap left, it went onto three cylinders and my heart was in my mouth. I realised I might have been getting low on petrol, so I knocked off 1,500 revs and took it nice and steady all the way home; but the Suzuki signalling was so good I knew precisely where everybody else was, particularly Rutter, and I knew I had enough time to spare to

TT 1979

get me back safely as long as the tank hadn't emptied. In the end I was genuinely surprised just how easy it had all been for me. And as for setting up new records, it never once occurred to me that I'd gone fast enough to do it. I realised, of course, I was on my way, but not that quick.

'When you think we might not have even been on the line for the start but for Martin and his merry men, it was all a terrific bonus and I was as pleased for them as I was for me.'

The next problem was to survive the night. Attwood, in his giant Mercedes, had done his damnedest to write us off on the way back from the grandstand after the race. He had not been allowed to have the keys to the car he had loaned us – for *his* protection as well as that of the *island*'s population – and in a rash moment of forgetfulness I handed them over to him so he could bring the ritzy limousine into the paddock to pick us up and take us home. The mood, as can be imagined, was one of whoopee and the BMW hospitality marquee had been a haven of kindness and boozy reward, with champagne flowing as if they had won the race themselves. In that spirit Attwood drove a car-load of Mike and me and friends back to town – with all the verve of his Le Mans days, but fuelled on champagne and encouragement from his tightly packed passengers.

There is a back road that climbs steeply up from the capital, Douglas, and winds treacherously through two arches under a viaduct into a blind bend. Going *up* from town is a gear-grinding, engine-testing climb. Going *down* Attwood style, as we discovered, left a good deal to be desired. He dived towards the archway in the left lane, found some wet leaves at the most critical point of the steep slope and slithered sideways alarmingly. Rather than clout the middle buttress, the stout grey stonework that suddenly loomed largely, he aimed the nose of our expensive motor through the right-hand archway – the up-line from Douglas, as busy a route during TT week as there is in the British Isles – and plunged through. It must have been the only five-second interval *ever* in the Isle of Man when nobody was coming the other way. Attwood, of course, put it all down to good judgement, fine control and eagle eyesight.

Mike

'Nothing to worry about, old chums,' he said blandly, his face greying. 'Just making sure you're all still awake.' Mike, who had just successfully and safely negotiated 226 miles of pitfalls and danger at every turn, put an instant driving-ban on Dickie for the rest of the week – and fined him heavily at the Round Bar celebrations.

For what was left of the week Mike pondered on the tough job ahead, his final appearance at the TT, the Classic – and he knew it would probably boil down once more to a direct confrontation with Alex George. He was right, and his worst fears were realised in a response that sent him racing over the limit he had set himself and far beyond any demands made on him. George was a man inspired, and Mike would not back off even when he felt he was sliding along a thin slippery line, separating safety from disaster by the narrowest of margins.

'If I'd thought it was going to turn out like it did, I would probably have never started the race,' said Mike later. 'I had to go into areas I had hoped I had long abandoned. There was no way I wanted to finish my Isle of Man racing career so close to the edge. I'm surprised that, at my age, I got myself involved in such a scrap. But I forgot all about the caution everybody had tried to drill in me before the race and instinctively went for it in as big a way as I knew how.'

The upshot was that the Classic TT of 1979 turned out to be just that – a classic.

'We had a bigger engine, a 652cc motor,' said Rex White, 'and it was super-quick. But Mike felt that the 500, the one he'd won the Senior on, was plenty good enough to do the business. So we stripped it and rebuilt it and it was as good as new. We realised it had all the capability to last the distance at the sort of hammer it was going to get; the bigger engine probably would not have gone the distance.'

'In that case they should have put that one in,' laughed Mike afterwards, 'it would have saved all the near-heart attacks I had trying to beat my way to the front.'

Whether Alex George would have been motivated enough to ride as hard as he did had it not been Hailwood he was facing is a question that has intrigued TT pundits ever since;

TT 1979

as it was he rode out of his skin. Perhaps, said Mike later, the £10,000 prize money fired him into a fury of action. 'I can't imagine how close to the edge he must have been,' Mike told me. 'I was over the limit all around the place and I know it must have been the same for him. He was like a man possessed – but all credit to the chap. I couldn't, or rather didn't want to, go any quicker.'

Against Mike's eager 500cc Suzuki George had been given Haslam's 998cc Formula One Honda, a thunderously powerful mount that obviously had the edge but still had to be ridden – and courageously too. There was no shrinking from that heavy responsibility by the Scot, who seemed to blossom in the raw challenge offered by the TT. It was clearly to be Mike's last TT and George realised the sentiment attached to it, but among racing professionals there is no room for that kind of emotion and Mike knew he would get none of it. Neither would he have wanted it; but if you cannot bow out with a win, there is only one other way to go – gloriously. And Mike managed to achieve that in an unforgettable finale.

'Not that I would have planned it that way. I thought I'd put all the nerve-racking business behind me after that big dice with Agostini in '67,' said Mike. 'An old man like me can't stand it. The old ticker, you know, it takes the zip out of the batteries in the pacemaker.'

He called me across as he sat impassively on the grid waiting for the countdown; Alex George, equally calm on the outside, and clowning with Mike only a few minutes before their titanic battle, was three places behind him on number nine. He shoved his helmeted face up against mine and shouted over the din: 'That bugger's going to go a bit, you know.' He pointed a thumb in George's direction, then added, 'It's about now I wish I was a window cleaner.' And with that he was gone.

At the end of the first lap, after $37\frac{3}{4}$ miles of sweated effort by George and a steadier rush by Mike to keep in touch, the Honda was stretching itself into a lead of 9.2 seconds. A lap later Mike had shaved off some of Alex's hard-won advantage, clipping a little more than 5 seconds off the lead.

Mike

They hurtled round lap three and in for the quick-fill petrol stops in exactly the same time, with George still fractionally ahead. They had covered 113 miles in less than an hour, the first time that had ever happened. The race was half over, but there were more fireworks to come in what had developed into a breathtaking two-horse race. On the fourth lap Alex was in front by 4.2 seconds, but a lap later, with one to go, Mike edged ahead by a blink – four-fifths of a second. It was all right for them – they had something to do, something to occupy them. For those of us sitting in the grandstands back at the finish line, there was only the commentary to listen to, the clocks to watch, the spasmodic feeding of information from the Suzuki radio watch around the course, and a bundle of nerves to try and settle by nail biting. Could Mike hold on?

On the last lap Mike held the lead at Ballacraine with nearly thirty miles to go. At Ballaugh, where the hump-backed bridge springs the bikes off the ground, he was still in front. Twenty miles left. The fight in his heart must have been a blaze of single-minded determination; but the will to win was just as alive in George's spirit. They were squabbling over flashes of time on the stop-watch, see-sawing, snatching the lead, having it snatched away. It was race drama at its most gripping, a tussle between two men who did not know the meaning of the words fear or surrender. At Ramsey, with nearly fifteen miles to master and the soaring 1,400-foot mountain of Snaefell to climb, the brute power of the Honda, twice as hearty as the Suzuki, had bulled once more into the lead. It was now or never for both men. Alex went for it. So did Mike. A backmarker, unaware of the monumental struggle developing around his patch of road, wandered into Mike's line. It was enough, momentarily, to fade the flat-out, headlong charge the Suzuki was being forced into. The backmarker had gone by the time Alex, behind on the road, swept through, unhindered, blasting his way towards the chequered flag. The party was over for Mike.

I waited for him at the finish. He pulled off his helmet. What hair he had was strewn about his ears, his eyes were

Above: *Giacomo Agostini on the MV 500-4. For a time he was Mike's MV team-mate, later he was one of his most skilful and tenacious opponents, as well as a good friend. His race on the MV against Mike's Honda 500-4 in the 1967 Senior TT, which only ended when the MV's chain snapped, is still considered one of the finest Seniors of all time.*

Right: *The Isle of Man TT Races, 1967. Mike shakes hands with ten-times TT winner Stanley Woods, whose record of wins he had just broken, while Stan Hailwood looks on. It was Mike's last TT before his comeback eleven years later.*

Right: *In 1971 and '72 Mike raced 3-cylinder 750cc BSAs at Daytona, but despite brilliant riding suffered machine failure in both years.*

Above: *Somehow car-racing never came right for Hailwood, despite some successes. In 1972 he won the Formula Two championship for Surtees. Here he is seen after coming second to Tim Schenken in Hockenheim, the second-to-last race of the season — that second place gave him enough points to clinch the championship.*

Above: *Mike's Formula One career improved dramatically when he joined the Yardley-McLaren team in 1974 — before that his Surtees-Fords had proved too unreliable. He is seen here in the Yardley-McLaren M23 during a Grand Prix, not long before his car-racing days came to a sudden end.*

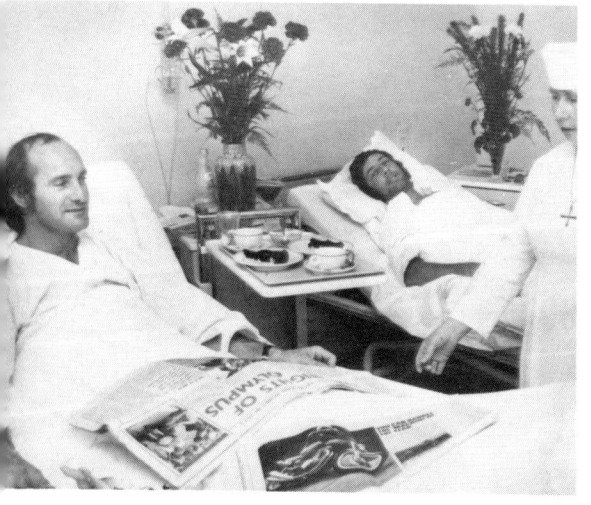

Left: *At the German Grand Prix at the Nürburgring in August 1974, Mike's Yardley-McLaren M23 hit the Armco at over 100 mph. The accident badly damaged his right leg and foot, and ended his Formula One career for ever. Adenau Hospital, with injured fellow racer Howard Ganley.*

Left: *The author, Ted Macauley (left), with Mike and mechanic Nobby Clarke during practice for the 1978 'comeback' TT. The strain is evident in Hailwood's expression.*

Above: *Strain or no strain, the magic had not gone and the 1978 F1 TT proved it. Hailwood on the 900cc Ducati (12) catches up with Read's Honda just before Parliament Square, Ramsey. Mike started 50 seconds behind on the road . . .*

Right: *And nothing Read or the Honda could do would prevent the one thing that thousands of wildly applauding spectators had come to see. Read looks round as Hailwood prepares to pass him, near the Bungalow in the 1978 F1 TT.*

Above: *Mick Grant, one of the greatest TT riders of all time and an admirer of Mike's, here on his way to his 1978 Classic TT win.*

Below: *Mike practising on the 1979 Ducati at Oulton Park before the TT. The factory's modifications had all but ruined the bike, and he did well to finish fifth in the F1 TT.*

Above: *Whatever the frustrations of the Ducati and the F1 race, Mike made the Senior his own. Here he comes through Creg-ny-Baa on the 500 Suzuki in the 1979 Senior, which he won at a record speed.*

Below: *After the 1979 Senior – Mike with the second- and third-place men, Tony Rutter (left) and Dennis Ireland, and the inevitable bottle of champagne.*

Left: *However good the Senior, the Classic proved to be one of the greatest races the Island has ever seen. Mike on the 500 Suzuki at Quarter Bridge, displaying a stylishness that has all but vanished – not for him the 'knee-out, backside-off-seat' style of today's racers. He lost to Alex George's much larger-engined Honda by only 3.4 seconds after 226 racing miles.*

Below: *Hailwood, Ted Macauley (centre) and Group Captain John 'Cat's Eyes' Cunningham, the famous wartime bomber pilot, at the presentation of the Segrave Trophy to Mike for his 1978 and 1979 TT exploits. The two heroes were delighted to meet each other, and Mike ensured that the Segrave Medal went to Macauley for the part he had played.*

Above: *Death of a legend. The wreckage of Mike's 3500 Rover after the accident on 21 March 1981. Michelle, his daughter, died instantly, Mike two days later; miraculously, David escaped virtually unhurt. Superb police work proved the lorry-driver's guilt, and established that Mike had been driving blamelessly.*

Left: *Pauline Hailwood arrives at St Mary Magdalene's Church, Tanworth-in-Arden, for the funeral, 31 March 1981.*

Below: *With the famous white, red and gold helmet on top, Mike's coffin is borne from the church by six pallbearers, among them Geoff Duke (left), Dickie Attwood (centre) and James Hunt.*

Mike Hailwood, MBE, George Medal, as he will always be remembered — a winner — seen here (top) on the eerily wailing Honda 250-6 in the sixties...

(centre) on the Sports Motor Cycles 900cc Ducati on which, against all odds, he beat Phil Read and the works Honda in the 1978 F1 TT...

And (opposite) after winning the 1978 F1 TT.

TT 1979

red raw, his face drawn and disappointed, and I think he knew before I told him the saddest news I'd ever given him in my life: 'You lost it by 3.4 seconds.' The countdown in the time-elapse was an agony of a wait, but Alex, who had ridden the race of his life to lick the maestro, had turned the algebra of racing at the TT into splendid achievement.

Alex had mixed feelings about beating Mike. 'I'd have given anything for it not to have been him, he's always been my hero, my idol, and I would have loved to have seen him quit the TT with a win. But I had a job to do. He understands. He knows. It's the saddest, happiest day of my life,' said the star who had completed with superb efficiency the job nobody really wanted to do. He bubbled: 'And didn't he make me fight for it? What a race! What a man! That will go down as one of the greatest TTs of them all – and I'm proud to have been able to play my part in making it so.'

Three-point-four seconds. Count it out. Watch it pass on your stop-watch. We did in the hotel. And we could not come to terms with that narrowest of margins after 226 miles of hell-for-leather dicing. 'Never again,' said Mike. 'I just feel lucky to have got away with it without getting hurt.' The supreme irony was that after all the years he had been racing at the frontline of TT action he had never suffered more than the cut finger after his 1978 250 tumble, and even though he had been off a couple of times he had escaped unscathed.

'Incredible, isn't it?' he mused, 'and when you think just what I have had to do here over the years with MV and Honda, with guys like Redman and Read and Ivy to beat, it's some sort of miracle. I'm only glad I didn't spoil my record this afternoon. I'd have hated myself if you'd been forced into a situation where you were smuggling vodka into hospital for me – vodka and surgical spirit! Let's try some. Let's try *anything*! It's all over and I have earned the right to get pissed out of my head.'

We had spent so much time together over the two years at the TT, and in between times, that Mike said: 'I wonder what people are thinking? I'll bet they've got us written off as a pair of poofters – we share bedrooms, eat together all the

Mike

time, booze it up shoulder-to-shoulder. Ah well, who cares what anybody thinks? At least *we* know we're okay. Let's go for a drink.'

The Round Bar was packed. Mike shouted for a vodka and lemonade for himself. All eyes settled on him. 'And a large brandy, Remy-Martin please, for my friend Edwina' – then he gave me a kiss on the cheek!

5

The Motor-Cycle Star

A year later Alex George recalled his bitter-sweet Classic triumph, the pinnacle of his racing career, and as the man who had won the fastest TT of them all – an average of 113.08 mph, for the 226 miles – he admitted he had mixed feelings about his glory day. 'As far as I was concerned,' he said in the 1980 TT programme, 'it was a privilege to have been in the same race as Mike, but to win was something else.'

Then he revealed: 'There were some worrying moments on the fifth lap of that race when the rear shocks started to overheat and were not working properly. It caused the machine to shudder badly on braking. And when I got a 'minus-one', a second down on Mike, it could not have come at a worse time for me. I was tired mentally and physically by then because the race was really tough and demanded immense concentration. I started to go to pieces and made a mess of Creg-ny-Baa, scattering the spectators. It was the same at Signpost where I nearly clipped the bank. And it was then, having had these near misses, that I said to myself "Alex, there's no sense in this, stop being silly, settle down and concentrate."

'The pattering was putting me off, so I decided I'd take

Mike

advantage of the 500 more revs I had been told I could use in an emergency, and boy, was this an emergency! I started to go quicker on the straights and take more care on the corners and I soon got back the two seconds. It was also on my mind that Mick Grant was going to race the bike I was on at Mallory Park the following Sunday – and that if I bent it he wouldn't be too pleased. Even as I crossed the line I didn't know who had won. People were shouting "two seconds" then "three seconds" and I thought Mike must have done it – and good luck to him – then when I was told I'd done it, I thought it was a big joke.

'When I realised it was true and I had won, I had a heavy heart because I had to beat Mike to do it. Despite the win and the great moment of my life, Mike the Bike is still the maestro and always will be so far as I am concerned. And, do you know, I never thought once about the money involved ... it was the happiest and yet the saddest moment in my life at the end of that Classic. I just wish Mike had stopped and that I had not beaten him in the way I did – after that TT race people were pointing at me and saying "He's the bloke who beat Mike Hailwood." Thankfully, after a couple of weeks, I seemed to become accepted for what I had done and was not considered a nasty man any more. People then started to say "Well done, you're a double TT winner." '

The follow-up Mallory Park meeting which drew another huge crowd was no action replay of the year before. Steve Wynne, full of apologies for the Ducati débâcle, suggested to Mike that there would be no point at all in trying on the Italian factory machine. Instead Mike was fixed up with a Mocheck Honda, and that was hardly equal to the task either. The upshot was that he had a dreadful weekend, struggled through a massive hangover, flu and general weariness after his TT efforts, and was well short of his best form.

He phoned me: 'That's it, I've quit racing. After Mallory I'm doing no more – I was sick the way it all went there and now I've had my fill.' I was staggered because I was relying on him making his finale at the *Daily Mirror* meeting at Donington Park, one of his favourite circuits. When I

The Motor-Cycle Star

reminded him and told him he could not just quit without having told anybody, he saw some sense in what I was saying; we agreed to make the formal announcement of his retirement at Donington Park's July 1979 international, so that the fans would have a chance to see him perform for the last time.

The response was gigantic. Everybody, it seemed, wanted to see Mike's final flourish, and bookings doubled, then trebled. I went off on holiday to Italy, confident that all was well, everything was organised and Mike's curtain-call at the end of his racing career was to give him the sort of farewell he, and everybody else for that matter, would remember for the rest of their lives. I asked him to call me in Tuscany after the race on Sunday and let me know how he had got on. Three days later there was still no phone call, though it was most unlike Mike to fail on a promise. So I rang him and, after a long conversation of triviality and small talk about the weather and the great benefit to mankind of holidays and how ready he felt he was to take one, he was finally cornered into revealing: 'I fell off. But I didn't want to spoil your holiday by ringing and telling you. I did my collar bone in on Saturday and couldn't race on Sunday. That's the bad news. The good news is that about 60,000 people came to see me not race.'

Tom Wheatcroft, Donington's rough-and-ready millionaire owner, a long-time fan of Mike, takes up the story. 'When I came to dealing with him for the meeting he was a gem. I asked him how much he wanted and he said how much did I want to pay. And I said we couldn't do business like that, he'd have to set a figure and I'd have to see if I could afford it. But he wouldn't do it that way — he produced bits of paper that showed how much he'd been paid at Mallory and I topped it. But he said he'd have raced for nothing, particularly as it was going to be his farewell, his party, and I know he meant it. I think the whole deal was settled in thirty seconds; there was no haggling or squabbling like with so many other buggers who have raced for me.

'I couldn't believe his appeal for people, not until I went

Mike

round in a helicopter with him on the morning of the first race – there were programmes and every hand in the place waving up at him. It was fantastic.

'In fact, the whole weekend was so incredible it was the best time of my life. I've done all sorts of things – raced and won three championships in one year, been a successful businessman, set up the finest race circuit in Britain, and enjoyed the company of all the world's great racers – but this was the best time of my entire life. I'll never forget it; to share it with Mike, to be part of it, and to have him on my track was just unbelievable.'

The year before, Mike had stirred Donington's thousands with a typical dashing display on the Ducati. 'He was leading by thousands of yards,' said Tom, 'and nobody had a hope in hell of catching him up if all went well for him. But it didn't; the bike went sick about the fourth lap. Next time round the lads behind had got a bit closer, then another lap and they were closer still. And typical of Mike he tried that bit harder to pull away. He went a good deal quicker at Coppice corner, didn't use his brakes, overdid it and the front wheel went from under and chucked him off.'

There was no reason to suppose the crowds would not get the same treat at his farewell party. But Mike tumbled in practice. Said Tom: 'And when I went to see him in the medical centre, he looked terrible. He'd done his collar bone and he was in a lot of pain. It was obvious he wasn't going to be able to race the day afterwards, his real big day, his last race, even though he would want to. We took him to hospital and he was in overnight after an operation to fix it. When we called to pick him up on Sunday morning, he was nowhere to be seen. He was at another fella's bedside, another racer who'd fallen off, and he was wishing him all the best and telling him not to worry; he'd be okay. And he himself was in terrible agony. We could see that. There was no way he could race and even though the radio was full of the news there were still 52,000 paying customers packed inside by the time we got there. The traffic jams went on for ever. Mike insisted on going to Donington, poorly as he was, and *still* agreed to sign autographs even though he was in a

The Motor-Cycle Star

lot of pain and looked very groggy indeed.

'It's a crowd that we have never topped – and I'm sure that if he had been racing, it would have nearly doubled to a Grand Prix size. It touched Mike very much and he asked if he could go round the circuit and give the fans a wave. He climbed into my eight-litre Bentley and we took him round. What a sight! What a noise! The place was packed and the atmosphere and affection generated made you feel warm – and it was all aimed at Mike. How he made it I don't know, he was really hurting, but he waved all the way round. That, for me, was the measure of the man. A man's man – no bloody bunkum about him.

'We found him somewhere to sit in relative comfort and he wouldn't go until nearly the end, about 3.45 in the afternoon, just before the crowds were set to leave. I gave him the money we'd agreed in a paper bag – £12,000 in cash. But he handed it back and said he wasn't taking it because he hadn't given full value! Can you believe that? He was turning down twelve grand. Well, there was no way I was having that, not even from him. I didn't argue about it any more, I waited until he wasn't looking and I gave it to his pal, Dickie Attwood, to take home for him and give it to him well away from Donington. We'd well and truly had our money's worth; he had turned it into the most unforgettable weekend any of us could remember – we'll certainly never see the like of it again. What he *was* happy to accept was a tea-service because it commemorated it as a special event, his last race. And he treasured it.

'A few days later I got a note from him, a real touching little note that *I* treasured. It just seemed to sum up the man's character and his appreciation of people's actions. I rank him alongside Fangio as a gentleman – but he was, and still is, my favourite man.'

Tom Wheatcroft took former Grand Prix racer Dan Gurney to the TT to see Mike's comeback race in 1978. 'When Mike went up on the winner's rostrum after winning the Formula One, we looked up at him, right up there on high where he deserved to be. I felt myself filling up and I looked across at old Dan Gurney. There were tears trickling

Mike

down his cheeks. It was a moment that stirred Dan into coming back himself the following year; he had stared at Mike, fagged out, looking like a man very close to collapse but so full of joy at winning, and he felt moved to give it a go again.'

Wheatcroft's deep affection for Mike found its outlet at his splendid museum at Donington Park, his race track in its superb rural setting near Derby in the Midlands. He set about collecting as many Mike memorabilia as he could – the Honda 500, the 350, and something like 400 of his trophies, 200 of them sent by Mike in an old tea chest and another 200 donated by Pauline Hailwood after Mike had been killed. He also battled to retrieve the famous Honda 250 Six which had found its way to Holland after Mike had written a promise to Tom that he could have it for the museum.

'I just wanted to put Mike's machines and Jock Taylor's in the museum and then turn it into a rather elusive, by-appointment-only centre,' he told me. Jock Taylor, the Scotsman who won the world sidecar championship and was killed in a tragic crash in Finland, was another of Tom's racing heroes and he had enough affection for the gentle Lowlander to rank him alongside Mike in the museum. As for that 250 Six, Wheatcroft, a determined man, said: 'I'll get it back in this country, where it belongs, as a fine memorial to Mike, at any cost. I owe it to Mike and his family.'

The last time I saw the famous Six and the infamous 500 Four, they were standing in Mike's beautiful home at Bray at Maidenhead, the big one in the dining-room, the lightweight in the porch. The kids played on them.

Mike could easily have harvested a fortune for them, but despite all the offers and the good and bad times he had enjoyed and suffered with the bikes, he had an affection for them which precluded him from taking up the bids. 'I want them to stay in Britain, and that's why I'd like them to go in Tom's museum,' he said, 'and that's what I intend to do with them.' He even turned down a £40,000 offer; it would, to him, have been like auctioning off his past and he was not prepared to do that. As much as he liked money.

Sponsor Steve Wynne's view, that he never appreciated

The Motor-Cycle Star

just how good Mike was until other riders and so-called superstars came under his wing or into his focus, is more than adequately supported by the variety of machinery which Mike rode and the success he had at all weights and capacities, whether two-stroke or four, and whether in Grand Prix, TT or short-circuit internationals.

His achievements are so well documented that to detail them would be almost an insult to those hundreds of thousands of fans around the world who can reel them off in a litany of appreciation; but for those who were late in joining the Mike Hailwood fan club, it is worth going over some of the ground he made so hallowed. It is greatness born, bred and developed into legend that at times baffled and bewildered the great man himself. Equally, while his relationship with his father, Stan, was not always one of peace and goodwill, he learned to understand that without his father's tremendous drive and motivation he might not have found the will to make the breakthrough; he could, instead, have languished in Stan's shadow, lapping up the good living and taking it easy. At least, that is a view offered by outsiders. However, Stan, I feel, would have found *something* worthy about his son, and I am sure that a talent as rich as Mike's would have burst clear of whatever confinements or constraints existed.

The petty jealousies which clouded his early career were soon wiped out when rivals realised that it does not matter if your father can afford to buy you the fastest machine in the world, you still have to ride it. Nobody can help you then. All Stan's money served to do was to get Mike to where he needed to be just that little bit quicker; there is no doubt he would have got there anyway. Stan's wallet may have been the accelerator, but that was all. When the blaze of Hailwood skill lit up the race world, it raged for twenty-two years of mammoth achievement, though the man himself hid behind a mask of modesty, reluctant to accept the accolades to a degree that was totally endearing.

His first race was on a borrowed 125cc MV single at Oulton Park, Cheshire, on 22 April 1957 – a little more than two weeks after his seventeenth birthday. He came eleventh.

Mike

Five days later he was fourth and fifth in the 125cc and 250cc races at a Castle Combe national, a truly remarkable start. But he topped even that inside two months when in front of 40,000 spectators he clinched his first win, in the 125cc class at Blandford; he followed it up with a third place in the 50cc race and a fifth in the 250. Four months later he had qualified for an international licence with four wins, three seconds, three thirds and three fourths in only eighteen races. But the pain of progress, a trap for the unwary, lay ahead and, after his international debut at Oulton Park had brought him a 50cc second and a 125 third, he fell off. He was chasing that other prodigy, John Surtees, in the 250cc event, but overdid his enthusiasm, was flung over the high-side and broke a collar-bone. By then the newspapers, not given at the time to airing too much news about motor-cycle racing, were heralding a wonderboy.

'Then Stan decided my education was somewhat lacking, so he sent me off to South Africa with Dave Chadwick. It was marvellous experience and we did quite well out there. It certainly toughened me up, put a bit more of an edge on my racing because I was just some bum English lad to them, somebody with more money than brains, a daddy's lad,' Mike told me, 'and I had to be shown what true life was all about.'

After that hard winter – 1957-58 – Mike returned to face his first season of world championship racing in Europe, and he was ready for action. But Stan felt he had not yet got Mike straightened out.

'He must have thought I was wrong in the head; I don't think I was giving him any trouble, not that I can remember, but he sent me to a Harley Street psychiatrist to get my bonce sorted out. It certainly puzzled me,' said Mike years later, 'and as he never bothered to explain it I didn't bother to ask. He'd have done better to have saved his money and sent me when I thought about going back to the TT after eleven years – the old shrink would have had something to work on then.'

Barely fourteen months after he had started racing, and still only eighteen years old, Mike was entered by Stan for

The Motor-Cycle Star

the TT; it was, of course, a world championship event in those days. It was to be the start of a Grand Prix career for the shy lad from Oxford. He had a brace of Nortons, a 350 and a 500, an NSU 250 and a 125cc Ducati, and a veritable barrage of publicity – the wonderkid versus the world's toughest course and some of racing's great men of the day. He acquitted himself perfectly, rode fast but with intelligent restraint and managed to finish all four races, which was a tribute to his sympathy for engines even at such a tender racing age. His best show was in the 250cc race, in which he was, astoundingly, third behind the works MVs of Tarquinio Provini and Carlo Ubbiali, in a race held over the now defunct Clypse circuit, ten and three-quarter miles of hard street-racing.

It was the stuff of which dreams are made; then there was seventh place in the 125cc race, twelfth in the Junior on the 350cc Manx Norton and thirteenth in the Senior. By the end of the season he had romped away with the British championship titles in the 125, 250 and 350cc classes and had made it into fourth place in the world 250cc championship and sixth in the 350cc class. The NSU had taken him into third place at the TT; it saw him home in fourth place at the Dutch TT – and then second in Sweden. The 350 Norton carried him to fifth place in Holland, fourth at the West German Grand Prix and third in Sweden. It was by any standard a brilliant start to a Grand Prix career. A year later he won his first world championship race, the Ulster at Dundrod, on a 125 Ducati. He had also moved a little closer to the crown, third in the championship for 125s, fifth in the 250cc class.

After only four years campaigning in the battle for world championship honours, he took the 250cc title in 1961 on a private Honda; he was also runner-up in the 500cc championship. The Honda, cleverly organised by his hard-working father, was second at the French Grand Prix, first at the Isle of Man and Dutch TTs, third in Belgium, first in East Germany, second at the Ulster and the Italian, and first again in Sweden.

He had been fourth on the 500cc Norton in Germany,

Mike

second at the French, first at the TT, second at the Dutch, the Belgian, the East German, and the Ulster, first again in Italy, this time on a 500 MV, and second in Sweden on the Italian flying machine.

'Heady days,' said Mike, 'and I was starting to realise just how much fun racing motor-bikes could be; there were so many fantastic fellas around I was having a smashing time. They were all so down to earth, no edge, no snooty buggers like car racing, and I felt right at home. Once they had got used to the idea that I was not Mr Moneybags and that I could hold my own, I was accepted for what I was – a motor-cycle racer.'

The mid-sixties heralded the halcyon days of racing. The week-by-week, season-long confrontations between Mike, Phil Read, Bill Ivy, Jim Redman, Frank Perris, Ernst Degner, Hugh Anderson, Alan Shepherd, Ralph Bryans and Tommy Robb, were as heart-stopping as they were exhilarating, races of hair-raising content, scary for those in them, hypnotic for those watching, neck-and-neck affairs in front of crowds as big as 300,000 in hotbeds of support like East Germany and Brno, Czechoslovakia.

Mike, fed up with his rationed appearances on the MV when, he felt, the real racing was being done among the lightweight men, the 250 stars who raced on the edge of survival, could not wait to get in amongst them. He even opted to ride the fickle but fast East German MZ until he could get into the Honda team. But finally that was arranged for him by Honda team-captain Jim Redman, desperate for help in fighting off Read and Ivy, in particular, on Yamahas that made missiles of the men on them.

Mike said: 'The heart of racing was in the 250cc class. It was tremendous stuff and I felt I was not getting in on it enough. The MZ outings, when I was in East Germany, only served to give me a bigger taste for the action. I was having a fairly easy time, I suppose, on the MV in the 500 class and I desperately wanted to join in. I must have been potty. Every weekend was heart-in-the-mouth stuff. No wonder I went bald. But I would not have missed it – to win one of those world titles was to know you had done something really

The Motor-Cycle Star

special. I knew I just *had* to do it. We were on the limit *all the time*, not just every now and then, *all the time*. It was all down to trust – faith in the other guy, no silly tricks, because there were rarely more than about twenty yards separating about eight of us, flat out and with those Suzukis, in particular, always likely to seize. "Whispering Death" we used to call them; they used to nip up so quickly and so often that their riders must have been nervous wrecks.'

Ulsterman Ralph Bryans, now a businessman in Ayr in Scotland, recalled how, after Mike had joined the Honda line-up, the team was assembled in Japan for testing. 'It was there, I suppose,' said the little Irishman, 'that I saw at first hand just how determined a character Mike was. He would not give up. Jim Redman was turning in some great times on the 250. Mike couldn't match them, but Jim was used to the bike and he knew his way round the circuit; even though the bike didn't steer too good, he had got the knack of it. I could see it was maddening Mike that Jim was so much quicker. His neck was swollen and red, his face was set and dead white, he was concentrating so hard and bursting with so much stubborn dedication to beating Jim's times. In the end he did.

'The next time I came face-to-face with this sort of effort from Mike was in Finland, when we were practising for the 250 Grand Prix. I'd got some super-quick times and Mike, trying really hard, couldn't work out how I was that much faster. We agreed to go out together so he could see where I was picking up and he was losing out and it soon became obvious what the difference was – I was so much lighter than him that I could get deeper on the braking and I got out quicker from the corners. Once he had realised what the difference was, he set about putting it right with sheer bravery and riding skill. He charged into the corner and went so deep I thought he was off. It scared me so much that I shut off and waited for him to start bouncing. But he was round, away and disappearing into the distance quite safely when I got through the corner. I couldn't believe what I had seen, so I made a big effort to catch him and follow him – and he did the same again for the next five practice laps. And

Mike

that's what made him so great. He was scared of nothing; he was both the bravest and most skilled rider I have ever seen. He would keep at it, like he did then at Imatra, until he had worked it out.'

Mike and Bryans, a rather frail and wispy-looking Irishman whose legs were about as meaty as pipe-cleaners, hit it off as pals right away. I know Mike appreciated the little man's intense determination, particularly when he viewed it over the awesomely testing Dundrod circuit near Belfast, scene of the Ulster Grand Prix. It always seemed to rain and, indeed, with typical Irishness, the circuit was set in a water-catchment area in the mountains behind that troubled city. Bryans, then a privateer, was a demon on his home ground and it was obvious to all that it would only be a matter of time before he was snapped up and recruited to join the 250cc fray. He revelled in the rain and was fast in the dry; the lightweights, the 250s, 125s and 50s, were his forte, and he could have weighed barely eight stone after the biggest of dinners. He and Mike were the unlikeliest pair, but they had open admiration for one another.

'We got on like a house on fire,' said Bryans, 'and I couldn't help but enjoy Mike's attitude. He was larger than life and didn't give a sod for anything, and if there was a bit of fun he was game. I can remember when Honda took us both to Japan at the end of 1967 – the year they quit – and paid us all our contract money in readies, in yen. We went on a spending spree, buying tons of stuff: cameras, radios, tape-recorders, anything to get rid of the money. Then we went missing. I'm not saying where or what we did, but for two days Honda couldn't find us. They were searching all over the place because we should have been on our way and gone from the country, but Mike insisted we had a day or two's fun. It was just a tremendous laugh to be with him.

'Though he wasn't *always* good humoured; there were days when he could be quite rude if something upset him or didn't go quite right. Usually, though, he stayed on an even keel; it was when anything went wrong with, say, the bike that he really got uptight. Anything out of his control which went wrong would needle him quite badly. It seemed to

The Motor-Cycle Star

stump him somehow, and if he was doing his best, trying his hardest, and he was let down by the bike, or somebody connected with it, then he could turn up with a rough side that you'd remember all your life. He could blast all right when he wanted to; most times, of course, he couldn't be bothered and he usually made up for somebody else's shortcomings through his fantastic ability.'

Once Mike had teamed up with Honda, he happily threw in his lot with wily captain Jim Redman, the London-born Rhodesian who took it upon himself to take care of the riders' problems and appearance-money wrangles. He was universally acknowledged as the master when it came to money matters; Mike, who really had little regard in those days for the wearing issues of arguing about cash, was content to leave it so that Jim would fix it. There was nobody better, nobody more fitted, and no tougher negotiator. Organisers who thought they had the Honda championship Grand Prix team in their pockets soon found out differently.

I remember Mike and Redman going into the race organiser's office at Brno before the Czechoslovakian Grand Prix. We had driven together in Jim's Mercedes, a 120-mph car with wonky steering, from East Germany, chased all the way by Giacomo Agostini in a Ferrari until he drove it off the road in a dream on the autobahn. The Honda team captain was in no mood to argue, and he told a rather smug official what his terms were for the team to race at Brno. This man, who had the crushing responsibility of making sure the world's finest racers turned up for the 300,000 thrill-starved fans, refused Redman's request. 'Right, Mike,' he said, 'let's go.' And he walked towards the door. He dared not really go through, nor dared Mike, because Honda's world championship survival was at stake. And I cannot imagine what would have happened if the nervous official had not called: 'All right Mr Redman, you can have what you want.'

They finished up with more Czechoslovakian money than they knew what to do with and had to stay on in Brno for two days after the race to spend it in a wild spree. They bought guns, cameras, watches and glassware, anything, to unload their crowns – and what they could not spend they

Mike

sold to other riders or journalists or trade helpers at a rate which would have got them imprisoned.

'The bloody Mafia would be hard pressed to do Redman on any sort of a deal,' said Mike. 'He's incredible. I don't know how he does it, but he does. I'm just happy to leave it all to him; he's a real hard nose in business. I couldn't be bothered.'

When there was only Bryans and Mike in the team – Redman had retired – they were shortchanged, they said, by the Dutch TT organisers. 'It was a terrible cock-up,' said Bryans, 'but Mike and I didn't get anywhere near the money we should have had. And we both felt that if Redman – Mr Fixit – had still been with us they wouldn't have dared to do us. He was worth his weight in gold to us all, a wheeler-dealer of the highest order.' I often wondered, watching Redman work so hard and so benevolently for his team-mates, if he was on a percentage. 'I'm bloody sure he was,' said Phil Read. 'Honda, with Redman looking after his lads, always used to get a better deal than anybody else. I wish he'd been looking after *my* interests.' Mike never revealed anything about the arrangements – he was plainly happy not to get involved in what he would consider to be the seedy side of the job of racing.

Bryans, a fiercely committed competitor who first met Mike – only to nod to – at the Isle of Man TT in 1962, got to know him deeply when they linked up together in the Honda line-up in the mid-sixties. And it was his selfless attitude, because of his affection for Mike, that gave Honda and Hailwood a 250cc world title in 1967 when Mike and Phil Read had dead-heated in the points total at the end of the year.

Ralph reckoned that he was retained in the team as a makeweight, a back-up for Mike in his bid to win the world 250cc title, until Honda produced a new lightweight that Bryans had been promised for 1968. But then the factory pulled out of racing and left both men in the lurch – even though they paid Mike a huge retainer *not* to race, not for anybody else, that is, for one year.

But in France, the third Grand Prix of the season, when

The Motor-Cycle Star

Mike and Phil had both broken down in the opening two rounds, Bryans made his sacrifice, partly because he feared that if he did otherwise he would lose his works ride and, more especially, because of his friendship with Mike.

'We were at Clermont Ferrand', said Bryans, 'and Mike's gearbox jammed. It left him trickling after Read and I caught him up. But I refused to pass him and, instead, let Mike get home in third place. I knew that he would need every point he could muster when it came to the final count-up at the end of the year. And I was right – the two of them dead-heated and it was all down, really, to the higher place Mike had over Phil's best placings.

'Mike couldn't understand why I stayed behind him and he said I should have gone on and licked him. He said "You should have gone for it yourself", but he still appreciated what I had done and he never ever forgot it.'

Neither did Read. 'If Bryans hadn't let Mike in, I would have been the champion,' he said, 'but that's the sort of affection Mike evoked in people all around him. And how can you beat it? My only regret in racing is that he had to be around when I was. I was pretty good, but he was better. It was so bloody frustrating knowing that I could beat most other guys – but Mike was a different case all together.

'But he always raced fair. He was never a dirty rider; I cannot recall him ever having done anything that threatened the safety of anybody racing against him. He was the true blue sportsman – thoroughly fast, braver than anybody and with a will to win that was frightening in its intensity. He would never cut you up, but if you left half an inch on either side, if there was the slightest hint of daylight, he was through it like greased lightning.'

Mike's fearlessness found its way into his off-circuit life too. That, and a boxing ability he had learned the hard way at Pangbourne Nautical College, where his father sent him in a bid to turn him into a public-school gentleman. What the college did was to turn Mike into a totally self-sufficient individual who hesitated to call on friends for help, and who would rather suffer the discomforts of deprivation than trouble anybody. His coolness, his athletic ability, his

Mike

strength and marvellous physique, and his reflexes turned into spectacular action when danger threatened either himself or his chums in those moments which all racing men seem to have – times which outsiders do not fully understand, any more than they appreciate the sense of fun and devil-may-care attitude.

Bryans again recalled: 'We were all down in Italy for a big international – Bill Ivy, Phil Read, Jim Redman and a pile of other guys. And we were in a nightclub on the Adriatic having a lot of fun, dancing and enjoying a superb floor-show. We just let the tab for all the booze keep on running – but at the end of the night the bill was horrendous. We argued about it, but it made no difference. We had slipped up and we just had to cough up. We all shared the outlay – but said we'd come back later on in the week.

'When we went back the night after, we decided to change the system and pay as we drank. And we thought we had mastered the problem, but we *still* were hit with a big bill at the finish. We argued it and refused to pay. We should have just cleared off, but we stayed on to argue the point. That gave the boss of the club a bit of breathing space and he rang round all the local hoods, and when we all eventually got out in the street it was full of his hard-case mates who were determined to kick the cash out of us. We had one hell of a set-to, a real mammoth battle. Mike, I remember, had some guy on the ground and was about to crack him when another Italian jumped on him and ripped the shirt off his back.

'When he got up and shook the guy off, Mike hit him so hard he broke a finger – he had to race at Brands the week after with it bandaged – and that was the only damage we suffered except for a fellow called Roy Robinson who used to pull Mike's caravan to the races; somebody whacked him with a starting handle. Mike was in the thick of it again in Argentina when a gang of local louts chased the bus carrying all the riders. They were chucking spark-plugs about and when the coach stopped everybody piled out and got stuck in and Mike was deep in the middle of all the action. And he was good ... bloody good! I'd rather have taken one clout

The Motor-Cycle Star

than two from him. Not only was he so quick, he could punch his weight.' In fact, at school Mike had had thirteen fights representing the college – twelve wins and one split decision – and by the time he had reached his early twenties, he was built like a middleweight. He worked hard to increase his strength and one of his favourite tricks was twisting soup spoons like corkscrews. I can recall him holding out at arms' length two of the massive, silver TT trophies; I could barely lift one on its own! He was hugely powerful; his upper chest, shoulders and forearms superbly developed even though he had spidery legs in comparison.

His physical development was paralleled by his riding prowess, even though in his twenties he was starting to take on the harum-scarum lifestyle which frequently puzzled the more dedicated followers of the sport. He was no playboy, not in the accepted sense where money means more than anything else and transcends the deep-seated desire to be best at what you do and what you have chosen as a career. His father made sure of that, for he was as down to earth, despite his wealth, as any coalface worker. And while he may have supported Mike with all the strength at his disposal, he most certainly did not spoil the boy, nor did he indulge the man. In fact, Mike told me he paid back huge amounts of money to Stan once he himself had started to earn a living from racing.

Stan's pride in Mike's achievements, and his own part in it, often embarrassed Mike. He was his number one fan, and he made sure that if anybody had any doubts about Mike's ability, then he would quickly, and forcibly, wipe those doubts out.

I can remember seeing him at the TT, sitting all alone on a bench behind the grandstand. Mike, riding an MV-Agusta, had climbed out of a sick-bed to race when, really, he should have still been tucked up in his room with an aspirin for company. Stan had a portable radio jammed up against his ear, listening to Mike's progress in the Senior, blissfully unaware of anybody else around him; he was worried sick that Mike, who had lost about a stone in weight and felt as weak as a kitten, should run into trouble. But he forbade me

Mike

from telling Mike – who, incidentally, won – that I had caught the old man in a vulnerable state of concern for his son's safety. 'Keep your bloody mouth shut,' he ordered. 'Anyway, if you tell him he'll never believe you. He thinks I don't care.'

It was only in later years that Mike fully appreciated what an ally he had in his father and what a staunch supporter he was.

It was later on that year, when we were all in Italy for the final Grand Prix of the season, that Stan turned up at Monza with a most beautiful teenage girl. He was spending that summer in a penthouse over a hotel in Cannes and the girl, who was anxious to get into films, thought the distinguished Stan, with his silver hair and pencil moustache, was a film producer. His silver Bentley Continental and his extravagant style did nothing to disabuse her of her error.

'You know what he did,' said Mike. 'He picked her up off the promenade, or whatever you call it, at Cannes. She was wearing only a bikini – but Stan wouldn't let her go home to get changed. He drove her all the way to Milan to watch me race, and she spent the time parading round in the smallest bikini I'd ever seen. She nearly stopped the traffic at the circuit. And I was bloody well ashamed of him – she was too young for *me*, never mind *him*. But I couldn't pinch her off him.'

It was a great source of sadness of Mike that Stan died in Miami before he could get to the Isle of Man to see that dramatic comeback. Mike had to fly to and from Miami and Barbados, where Stan had set up home after living in Nassau and on the Riviera, and sort out his family problems before he could start getting himself organised for the TT.

'I only wish old Stan could have seen the TT,' he said, 'He would have loved it. He was always right behind me when I needed him and I don't suppose I fully appreciated it until too late.'

Mike's depth of feeling for Stan showed itself quite touchingly when he dedicated his last win on the island to his father, in a public display of affection from the stage at the prize presentation. Stan was never really far away when

The Motor-Cycle Star

Mike was in full flight, and I am sure too Mike felt his untimely death from cancer far more deeply than he revealed.

I am sure it must have been Stan who taught Mike the trick of carrying only £20 notes with him, particularly when taxis had to be paid for, but that was mainly a joke.

It was a fight most times to pay dinner bills ahead of Mike and his generosity towards friends was limitless. One couple in particular had enjoyed his kindness, principally because he loved their company and was relaxed with them. Then, he said, he found the wife's script was the same week-in week-out, and it had become a little wearing. Gradually, bored by the same old stories, he ran down the frequency of the get-togethers. But then he met up with them in the dining room of a big hotel at a race and we all sat down together. The same, repetitive anecdotes and now-unfunny stories were prattled out and I could see Mike's eyes going dead in the onslaught. They flashed wide and bright when the wife, full of too much of Mike's hospitality, said: 'About time you bought a meal, Hailwood, you're always poncing on us.' He asked for the bill, paid it, and walked off without a word, and I doubt that he either sought them out or spoke more than a token formally good-mannered greeting to them from that day until the day he died. 'If it was a joke,' he said, 'it was in bad taste. If she was serious, then why should I bother to spend any time at all with such an ignorant drunk? Either way, their time is up.'

He could be hurt by unwarranted attacks, usually by people who knew no better and did not know him at all; but most times he would give as good as he got, caring not whether his target could take it. And there were a good few who did cross him who were dismissed from his life with a perfunctory word or two and who rarely made it back into his circle. They were usually rather less than scrupulous, so-called friends who took advantage of Mike's easy generosity to rifle either his pocket or his personality to their own distinct advantage.

In 1961 Mike made TT history and the eyes of the racing world, particularly the Japanese, were focused on his

Mike

achievement: three TT wins in one week and nearly a fourth but for a broken gudgeon-pin which would have cost about ten pence. He had hammered the superstars of the day in the 125cc class, Luigi Taveri and Australian Tom Phillis, who were riding carbon-copies of his little Honda. Then, in the 250cc race, he outpaced Phillis and Jim Redman on another Honda. His arch rival, the brilliant Gary Hocking, broke down on the MV four in the Junior 350cc class and Mike, aboard an AJS 7R, fronted the field until that pin surrendered his race for him on the last lap. He had better luck in the Senior. Again Hocking's MV hit trouble and Mike raced home to victory at an average of 100.60 mph.

It was one hell of a year for Mike, the turning-point of what had started to become an illustrious saga. His private Honda beat the works bikes of Phillis and Redman to the world 250cc title – his first. And in the 500cc class he stayed almost a hand's reach behind Hocking for the entire season: the MV four took the Rhodesian to the title, but Mike's reliable Manx Norton carried him to a fourth place in West Germany, a second in France, that win at the TT, and second place in four successive races in Holland, Belgium, East Germany and at the Ulster Grand Prix.

The shrewd Count Agusta, no doubt alerted by letters from Mike's father, saw the Hailwood genius was ready to flower and that it could be nurtured on one of his magnificent flying machines, the scarlet MV. It was a nervous Mike, with his father alongside, who waited in the outside office of the MV factory ... and waited ... and waited. The aristocratic Count Agusta may have wanted Mike in his team, but he had to exert his authority and had to let it be seen he was all powerful, all mighty in the sport.

'I was bloody well fed up of hanging around,' said Mike, 'and I wanted to leave. I got up to go, in fact, but remarkably the door to the inner office suddenly opened and we were summoned to appear before the great man. By then, I'd had enough, but old Stan kept me in check. We'd been there all day with nothing to eat and I was furious.'

The upshot of the marathon wait was the offer of a ride on the works MV for the Italian Grand Prix at Monza, the first

The Motor-Cycle Star

time Mike had been involved in the full works treatment – and he never looked back. He finished runner-up to Hocking in the 350cc race and won the 500 after the dapper little 'Socks' Hocking had taken a tumble. It meant that Mike had amassed enough points to give him second place in the 500cc championship. His MV future was assured and he totally dominated the series from 1962 until 1965, collecting four world titles.

The 350 MV was a totally different proposition; it was outclassed by Jim Redman's Honda and, despite some titanic battles between the two great friends, the Japanese factory took the title during the same period that Mike was triumphant in the blue-riband section. Then, at Redman's insistence, Honda moved in.

He had seen Mike's boredom with his total domination of the 500cc class on the unbeatable MV-Agusta, and not even his races against the clock, when there was little else to challenge him, could compensate for what he felt he was missing in the other events. Records, both lap and race average, tumbled in the face of Mike's thrust on the MV and he made every Grand Prix a one-man show of spectacular achievement without rivalry. But it was not enough. Redman had chosen his time to move with the same cool perfection he had displayed in his weekly 350 battles with the restless Hailwood. It was Redman at his most adroit, and Mike proved a willing recruit.

Even more world titles flowed at the twist of his right hand. He was first home in ten out of twelve Grand Prix races on the 250 in 1966. He beat the new Italian hero, Giacomo Agostini, Mike's former back-up rider with MV, for the 350cc crown. And then did it all again a year later, despite fierce opposition from Phil Read and Bill Ivy on their Yamahas and the close attentions of men like Alan Shepherd, Frank Perris, Hugh Anderson, and other fine performers of the calibre of Tommy Robb and Derek Woodman, the MZ specialist. He just could not, however, recapture the title he had almost made his own property, the premier 500cc championship. And little wonder; the big Honda was quite *the* most frightening machine ever

Mike

assembled. And any critical remarks levelled at it would go nowhere near adequately describing its hellish vagaries and intimidating waywardness. It scared the life out of Mike, but he could not resist the challenge it presented, nor could he back off from the infinite threat and danger it exuded with every blast from its four pipes.

'It'll be the death of me, that big Honda,' said Mike. 'It won't go in straight lines and it's like a concertina, it flexes so much. And when you're having to go like I'm having to go, it's bloody terrifying. I'll tell you something else; the way these Hondas, *all* of them, handle has proved to me what a great rider Redman must be. Even when they were swinging about all over the place, Jim was still going like a dingbat – I don't think he realised how bad they could be; he thought it was natural and that all bikes handled that way.'

Mike, who had shocked the conservative Japanese from their smug confidence about the unbeatable Hondas with a dismissive 'It's bloody awful' remark about the 250 when he first rode it at works level, battled on. He could tame the other bikes, but the 500 was like some wild, bucking, uncontrollable beast with a mind of its own. And if ever there was a great triumph over doubt in racing, it had to be Mike's hard-fought victory over Agostini's MV in the 1967 Senior TT. It was titanic stuff, with the lead constantly swapping, ranging over split seconds for the entire 226-mile struggle. Here were two men at an absolute peak of their form: Agostini, who had learned all his TT tricks from the master, and Mike, who was trying to introduce new plans for both survival and success on a machine which insisted on behaving monstrously. It developed into probably *the* greatest Senior of them all and certainly ranked alongside Mike's stirring duel with Alex George in the 1979 Classic as one of the most dramatic Isle of Man races of all.

Mike ran out the winner when the MV, not the man, gave up the ghost. The chain broke up and shredded itself like shrapnel, maybe a merciful release at a time when both men were riding outside the limits of what was safe and acceptable, living as dangerously as it was possible to live. With so much determination on display at such speeds, the

The Motor-Cycle Star

outcome could have been disastrous.

Mike told me later: 'What a race that was! I wouldn't want to go through another like that – I was scared all the way. Ago's MV obviously handled that much better than the Honda and I was fighting it on every lap. I knew Ago would give it his all and I knew I had to make sure he didn't get away and, if possible, stay in front. But even though I expected it to be pretty bad, I didn't expect it to be a nightmare. There's not enough money in the world to make me go through that again. If Ago hadn't broken down, I doubt that I would have beaten him, he was brilliant.

'Something else too. It showed what a cool character he is; he took the breakdown philosophically and with just a shrug of the shoulders. He might have been disappointed, but he didn't go on about it. Once he was back at the hotel he'd got over it – on the surface, that is. I'm more Latin than he is, I think; I'd have gone berserk. Not him. Dead calm. It's like we've been swapped over. He has the traditional English acceptance of something gone sadly wrong. I go crazy.'

I saw that at first hand in Italy later on in the year when, again, the Honda had given Mike a terrifying trip around Monza in a bid to wrap up the world 500cc championship. He had been riding brilliantly all year to compensate with courage and daring for the Honda's lack of steadiness, but in the final analysis, in Italy, with 100,000 partisan fans ranked against MV-deserter Hailwood and supporting home-hero Agostini, the Honda's gearbox churned itself to a standstill and the crown was Giacomo's.

The crowds were streaming from the Monza Autodrome when Mike drove me in his car back to our hotel – and it was quite the most terrifying drive I had ever had. Normally he was rock steady and unflustered on the road and brought none of his Grand Prix dash with him; but this time he was in a rage of disappointment and was swinging the car recklessly in and out of the crowds, sliding off the tarmac onto the grass to get through in one swoop when the way ahead was blocked or the traffic was at a standstill.

It was like that all the way back to the hotel and I must have spent most of the journey, nearly forty-five minutes,

Mike

cowering low in my seat or with my eyes firmly shut. He never said a word. And he lay in the darkness of the room we were sharing in total silence, letting the abject disappointment ebb away until it had cleared his system. It was his feeling, I gathered later, that he had done *his* level best and performed to *his* peak and the let-down was no doing of his. We enjoyed a good party that night, and he sent a case of champagne across to the mechanics who were sharing his upset just as deeply in a quieter corner of the hotel dining-room. And when he took me to the airport the following morning, having to get up at 6 am to drop me off, he was most apologetic about his behaviour. And the old smile was back on his face; perhaps because he had no more Grand Prix heart-stoppers to face.

It is worth recounting that when his full-time motor-cycle racing career closed at the end of 1967, he had won seventy-six Grands Prix, had been runner-up twenty-five times, third eleven times, fourth twelve times, fifth nine times and sixth twice; he had been inside the top six 135 times in world championship competition. The bewildering array of machinery he had ridden in international competition so gloriously and with such a mixture of affection and apprehension included: Mondial, AJS, NSU, Ducati, Norton, MZ, EMC, MV and Honda. Thirty-seven GP and TT victories were on 500s; sixteen on 350cc machines; twenty-one on 250s and even two on tiny 125s.

He had one or two forays back into two-wheel competition before his 1978 and 1979 TT comebacks. He competed in a 250 race at Silverstone on a Yamaha that would hardly pull your grandmother off her feet, and had two Daytona outings. He rode a BSA triple F750 machine there in 1970, qualified at 152.9 mph, second fastest on the grid to Gene Romero's 157.34 on a Triumph, and then led the race for twelve laps until ignition problems stopped him. A year later he was back again. This time he and Paul Smart and Gary Fisher, Triumph and Honda 750s respectively, battled it out for the lead until Mike's BSA suffered pushrod failure.

Mike had enormous affection for Daytona. It was not just

The Motor-Cycle Star

the racing at the Florida 200-Mile classic; the atmosphere suited him and he always seemed to enjoy a near TT-type feeling about the place. He was certainly relaxed whenever we were there together – and particularly the last time, just before he died. It was a zany place, and so full of crackpots and oddball people that it seemed to stir up in him all the mischief, ever-present but kept mostly in check as he got a little older and, as he said, a little more responsible.

At Daytona it was the rent-car companies that seemed to suffer most of all in those madcap days – the reversing races, with gas-guzzlers charging backwards and side-by-side; the how-far-can-you-drive-into-the-sea challenges; and will-it-go-into-reverse-at-60-mph-tests. It was all irresponsible stuff, but at the time, when the lifestyle was Battle-of-Britain, here-today-gone-tomorrow, it seemed the most natural way to be. And Mike was as much part of it as his outrageous pal Bill Ivy, the pocket Hercules famed for standing on his hands on moving curling stones across the ice at St Moritz, with the rich and famous of the jet-set looking on in total bewilderment.

I can recall Mike getting terribly worked up at some ill-mannered treatment he had been suffering from a car-rent company in Florida. He spent most of the week plotting how to make his point. He parked the troublesome car, an automatic, at the rental lot at the airport, then flew off home to London. But he had left it in first gear with the hand-brake locked firmly on and the engine running. It wasn't going anywhere, but the back wheels spinning, marking time on the spot, soon sent up plumes of threatening black smoke, while the tyres, grinding into the gravelly surface, were reduced to slicks in no time at all. Mike phoned up when he returned home to make sure the company had discovered his parking place – the answer was something like: 'Yes, Mr Hailwood, and we got the message okay too.'

Our last Daytona trip, in 1981, at least leaves me with the happy and contented feeling that the final get-together we had, the last time I ever saw Mike, was a hilarious episode that neither one of us, we said, would ever forget. As we split

Mike

up at Heathrow, London, after the flight back, we shook hands and he said: 'We must do it again next year.' And he walked away grinning hugely at the memory of it all. It was my last sight of him, and the smile on his face will always be with me, more especially because I feel I contributed to making his last days a joy, at a time when business difficulties were getting him down.

We had flown from Miami in a high state. There had been an afternoon spent doubled-up with laughter – no doubt due in some way to the red wine – in a downtown restaurant, waiting for the Jumbo home. Then an invitation to the British Airways lounge enabled us to lower their vodka stocks a little until we were loaded onto the big jet. We had noticed that the drinks trolley had been slow to get to us on the outward journey, so we had made our own arrangements and brought a couple of bottles of claret and a corkscrew to see us through that interminable wait until the plane is airborne and the bond is unlocked to free the booze.

British Airways had blocked off one seat in our row of three, so we had a vacant plot between us – elbow room, as it were, for two dedicated drinkers. Mike quickly got to work with the corkscrew and a sympathetic and understanding stewardess found two glasses to attend our first bottle.

We raised the glasses in a toast, clinked them together and settled down to enjoy the inevitable bliss that was sure to follow. Mike had put the freshly opened bottle on the tray in front of him – and suddenly it shot towards him, gushing red wine all over his white pants, and just about emptying itself into his lap before he could grab it. The old reflexes had been sabotaged by the day's events, and he was soaked. A woman had thrown herself hard into the seat in front of us, and the jolt had sent the bottle spinning off Mike's tray. He pointed out what had happened, but she did not even attempt an apology. He was as mad as I have ever seen him – and drenched, too. So he moved into the seat next to mine, still seething, and put what was left of the bottle in front of him. And she did it again! What had missed Mike first time round got him this time. I had to hang onto his arm to stop him saying his considerable piece to this somewhat

The Motor-Cycle Star

obnoxious American woman, who seemed to be trying hard to wreck our carefully laid plans; I was never entirely sure whether Mike's anger was because of her rudeness, his drenching, or that she had caused a drastic depletion of our stocks. She was so good-looking, and so elegantly turned out, that just one smile from her would have soothed the issue, and probably earned her an invitation to join us. But as there was nothing forthcoming in that line, Mike opted for revenge and, as always, it was sweet when it came. It took some time – we had not yet taken off – but it came ...

We must have been flying, in every sense of the word, for about an hour when the Jumbo turned a degree or two and went up another level. And as it nosed higher a rather expensive Gucci shoe, red and with a neat stiletto heel, came sliding towards us from the seat in front. Mike and I looked at it, then at each other, and smiled the way that people do when opportunity presents itself. Its owner, having kicked off both her shoes, snoozed not at all fitfully in the next row, without realising she was light by one Gucci. The shoe, like an old and valued friend, stayed with us for the rest of the night, until the breakfast trays and their rolls and sticky marmalade arrived ninety minutes out of London. By then the toe-end had been stuffed with soap which, watered and made slimy to fit, had then, of course, hardened as it dried. The marmalade, Frank Cooper's Oxford Thick Cut, was smeared about liberally where the ball of the delicate little foot would fit, and the shoe was then prodded back to its original resting place, ready for its first, halting steps on British soil.

What had started out as a neat size four had now been reduced by two sizes, but with that fearsome determination women have when it comes to style, our friend was crushing her right foot into a fashion plate shoe which was clearly not going to take it. Not with any comfort, that is. And we watched her hobbling along the concourse, no doubt thinking that all the airline warnings about the feet swelling at such high altitudes were true – but could they have grown so much? Mike, his pants still blotted with claret, and I were holding on to each other and giggling like St Trinians kids,

Mike

helpless at our trivial and juvenile revenge, when she turned and saw us. And if ever you saw a moment of realisation dawn on somebody's face, it was at 8.30 am that Tuesday morning in March; she did, at least, have enough in her to grin back at the secret which she now shared.

6

The Full Genius

John Cooper, the bespectacled racer from Derby, a man famous for his beating of Giacomo Agostini in an epic Mallory Park battle in the sixties, was once invited by Mike to join him for a holiday at his beautiful new home in Durban, on the South African coast.

Mike had set up a building business with his former Suzuki rival Frank Perris, but it did not go well and the partnership was folded after only a couple of years. Perris returned to England. Mike stayed on, but he still liked to have contact with his old chums and that is why he invited the down-to-earth Cooper to fly out and stay with him. In fact, 'Moon-eyes' Cooper was one of a whole string of racing friends who were only too happy to call in on Mike and enjoy his superb, if sometimes hair-raising, hospitality. His pool parties and, shall we say, lively and adult get-togethers were the gossip of the racing scene. Agostini, another caller at the Hailwood spread, never got over his trip: 'Fantastic,' he said, 'incredible. All those girls. And no clothes! I never had such good parties in my life.'

Cooper had been at the house barely a couple of days when he got Mike worried by turning redder than a lobster. Mike said: 'Old John had never seen as much sunshine and

Mike

he was determined to make sure he got all he could while it was going. I think he thought it wouldn't shine for much longer so he stayed out in it all day, and it was a killer. We tried to tell him it would be shining for the next ten months, but he wouldn't have it, he sat stoically by the pool getting more scarlet by the hour. I had to ban him from sunbathing.'

While they were there, Cooper and a friend were shown a telegram by Mike. 'It was ages old,' said John, 'and it was from Benelli. They wanted Mike to ride for them. Anybody else in the world would have jumped at the chance. Not Mike. And he said "Perhaps I'd better reply soon."

'It must have been a couple of months at least since they'd sent him the telegram and it was still in his drawer, almost forgotten. I couldn't believe it, but Mike couldn't care less. He was only worried that Benelli might think him a bit bad-mannered because he had not found time to answer.'

The Italian factory's boss, Nardi Dei, had watched Mike race 350 and 500 Benelli fours against Agostini's MV in a big-money series in Italy in the early seventies – it was the cash, not a furthering of his career, which had tempted Mike back into the motor-cycle fray – and he was most impressed. So he offered Mike what was then a huge contract to take up his offer of a works ride.

The lure was £30,000 a year, and in those days that was big money indeed. I can remember Mike telling me about it at the time, and as he was at a low point in his car racing he was almost tempted back into the saddle. Benelli at the time were bidding to outshine MV-Agusta and they had even offered Agostini a fat fee to join them. 'I'll bet he used the offer to get a big pay rise out of Count Agusta,' Mike told me. The money, while it was tempting, was never the complete and only attraction for Mike, and even though he enjoyed being rich, and being offered chances to be even richer, he much preferred having a good time and trying to avoid as much pressure as he could. He had been forced to live with pressure, one way or the other, all his life – through his father, his own teenage genius, and his works responsibilities – and now, in the early seventies, he did not want any more of it.

The Full Genius

When the Benelli offer came, right out of the blue, he told me: 'The offer was terrific – and they promised to develop new machinery, 350s and 500s, to beat the MV. Not only that, but they promised to put me in charge of the racing department. I'd have been the boss, controlling development and reserach and organising the racing and operating as the number one rider with a support rider if I felt it was necessary. It was a really great opportunity, but somehow I didn't feel the need to take such a big step.

'One of the main problems was that I'd been out of racing as a serious contender for nearly three years. Agostini, who would have been my main rival, was at the top of his form and he had been racing regularly and successfully. He was obviously on a big high – and I would be an old rustbox in comparison. I didn't think, quite honestly, I could do it, or justify that much faith in me. I was still only thirty, but I'd been out of top-flight racing three years and I reckoned the gulf between Ago and me would have widened so far that I'd have to stick my neck out too much to bridge it. You don't come back in this business, do you?'

His words seem now, in the light of his TT performances eight years later, to have been ridiculously ill-chosen. But it was his honesty that was working, not his greed. He genuinely believed he could not live up to his reputation, and so do the sort of job Benelli desperately wanted.

'It was common sense that had the upper hand,' he said, 'and despite all that lovely money on offer I had to turn it down. The pressure, I know, would have been right back on me. There could have been no racing for second place or putting up a decent show and finishing among the also-rans; it had to be a place on the victory rostrum, as the winner, and I couldn't give them that sort of guarantee. Maybe it might have been different if Benelli had come in a couple of years earlier, but I don't know. I still had the pull of motor-bike racing then, even though I wanted to get out and into cars and prove my worth in something completely different. Honda had gone a long way to souring me, particularly in that final year on the 500. That was too much. So Benelli, I'm sorry to say, suffered the knock-back.'

Mike

By the time he quit, Mike had been earning around £40,000 a year from Honda, about the same wages as he had been paid at MV. The only difference, of course, being that he had had only two rides with MV – the 350 and 500 – while at Honda he was having to chase three titles – the 250, 350 and 500.

'And I reckon they got their money's worth out of me,' he told me. 'That was heavy duty. It was fun in the 250 and 350 classes – the 350 was like a kitten compared with the 500 – but the senior class was hell. When they realised I couldn't win the 500cc title for them, they pulled out. They had done everything to pump more power into that 500, and all they did was pull it to a standstill in a development sense. MV did it all right and they got away with their new-found power because they had a frame that could handle it, experts who knew how to deal with it and not a load of Japanese insisting that if you had the power then how could you fail to win?

'In many ways Honda did me a favour by quitting underneath me. I'd felt at my very best form when I was racing in the 250 class – that was the greatest racing in the history of the sport – but after twelve years of non-stop action I think I'd had enough and was ready for the change. In fact, I was heartily sick of it all. There was nothing left for me in the sport, except to win the 500 title for Honda and that was out of the question. If it had gone on much longer, I'd have probably killed myself in the effort. I'd done everything else, championships and TTs, records and titles all over the place, so what else was there? Nothing. And the beauty, of course, was that Honda decided to pack it in for a while and still pay me for the rest of my contract provided I didn't race for anybody else. That was wonderful, a little pension in its way. I was happy to see the back of that 500. That bike was as much a challenge to me in any race as all those chaps lined up trying to beat me: I had to master that problem before I could get down to sorting out the others. What a way to go racing! No thanks.'

He smiled: 'There were times when I wasn't so sure whether I'd be going home in my car or in an ambulance. It really was that hairy. I finished runner-up twice in the 500

The Full Genius

class in 1966 and 1967 behind Ago's MV. And I put him into second place in the 350 class in the same years with my Honda. The difference between the battles for the two titles was immense; the 350 was a piece of cake. The 500, well ... I felt as if I was on a suicide mission.'

When Mike rode the Honda 500 to TT victory in 1967 and left the legacy of a Senior record for years afterwards, the throttle grip was sliding about the end of the bars and threatening to drop off, held on only by a mechanic's handkerchief. I could hardly appreciate the bravery that it must have taken to stay with it and not surrender. And when he gave Agostini an eleven-second start on the fourth lap and pegged him back so strongly that he reversed the deficit to take a one-second lead, I understood the full genius of the man. It makes the hair on my neck stand on end even now when I think back to that memorable afternoon.

'I knew Mike would not surrender anything,' said Agostini, 'he would not know how to give up. It was always the same and to beat him, ever, if only once, is a memory you could live on for the rest of your life. No wonder Alex George was so excited when he beat Mike in 1979 at the TT. I know his feelings.'

In 1968 Mike Hailwood was awarded the MBE in the Queen's New Year's Honours list, and when an Italian journalist asked him what the initials meant, Mike told him, without a trace of a smile, 'Motor-Bike Engineer'. The citation hung on the wall of his flat near London Airport with a sticker across it that read 'What a load of cobblers'. But secretly he was delighted – he was happy that he could bring to his sport a level of universal respectability which had not been too much in evidence since the era of Geoff Duke.

The George Medal which he won for rescuing Clay Regazzoni always embarrassed him and he would refuse to talk about it; but he loved being awarded the Segrave Trophy after his TT exploits in 1978 and 1979. So many other famous men before him, in totally different worlds, had had their names inscribed on it. Malcolm and Donald Campbell, John Cobb, Geoff Duke, Stirling Moss, Jackie

Mike

Stewart and even flier Amy Johnson – Mike appreciated that he was in illustrious company. I had no idea at all, but he nominated me for the Segrave Medal that went with the Trophy.

The letter from the Castrol-sponsored Segrave Trophy committee said: 'Former world motor-cycle champion Mike Hailwood, fourteen times a Tourist Trophy winner, has been awarded the Segrave Trophy for 1979 following his comeback in which he won the Senior TT and was only narrowly beaten into second place in the Classic TT.

'Announcing the award, Lord Camden, Chairman of the Segrave Committee, said the Trophy, which is awarded annually to the British subject who accomplishes the most outstanding demonstration of the possibilities of transport by land, air or water, was being given to Hailwood "for a classic farewell to TT racing in winning the Senior event and gaining second place in the Classic – and for his immaculate attitude which has set a fine example to all youngsters taking up the sport".'

It went on: 'In addition to the Trophy, a Segrave Medal is to be awarded to Ted Macauley as, says Mike Hailwood, "without him it would not have happened".' My medal, really awarded by Mike and therefore among my most treasured possessions, stands alongside three of the TT replicas he gave to me after the Isle of Man comeback, the helmet he wore in his Classic battle, and an obscene message to Mick Grant when Mick asked me, in Mike's hearing, to manage him for the following season.

At the presentation in the RAC headquarters in Pall Mall, London, Mike was almost overawed at meeting Group Captain John 'Cats Eyes' Cunningham, the famous RAF Pathfinder pilot. The wartime bomber hero, a shy and reticent man, was equally thrilled to meet Mike, and they asked each other for their autographs. It was the only time I had seen Mike, despite having been in the company of hundreds of world-famous people throughout his life, ever ask anybody to sign his name for him. 'I know how they feel,' he said. 'I get fed up sometimes, though I know I shouldn't, signing autographs. It can be bloody embarrassing.' Mike was so pleased

The Full Genius

with his daring in crossing to the Group Captain to get him to sign his programme that he asked for one for me as well. I do not think he asked for an autograph even when he was filming with Paul Newman, the car-racing film star, in a Le Mans 24-hour sequence. Though he did once have his picture taken with Hollywood singer Jack Jones – and he looks shrivelled with embarrassment in the photo, even though it was a Jones request.

Outside motor sport it was musicians who impressed Mike most of all. There was something of a jazzman inside him, bursting to get out; his skill with the piano, drums, clarinet and guitar, was self-taught, and he loved to play whenever he could. But never in public, and the only time I can recall him making music with more than three people around was at a party he threw at his home in Maidenhead. Then he sat in with the Chris Barber jazz band and thumped the drums and blew his clarinet all night long. He always said they only let him join in because it was *his* party in *his* house – like the kid who owns the ball who wants to be captain of the football team. And in Holland once, years ago, he sat up all night – insisting that I stay to get musically educated – to listen to a truly marvellous pianist who owned the hotel in which we were staying. That he was racing in a critically important Grand Prix only hours later did not matter to him. 'It's the best way I know to relax,' he argued. 'I just wish I could play like that.' The pianist, a race fan and Hailwood worshipper, would have swapped talents any time.

We went back to the same hotel in Assen in 1980 and the same man was still in charge, and still playing the piano so superbly well. Mike had insisted we stay there while he was earning a few pounds making a noisy demonstration ride on the refurbished 250 Honda Six for the 130,000 fans at the Dutch TT. As soon as the hotel owner saw Mike walk into the piano lounge, he picked up a George Shearing tune, one of Mike's all-time favourites, and it was as if no time had elapsed between the two trips, so far apart in reality. Much as Mike appreciated the man's memory, his talent, and his delight in seeing his hero again after such a long time, he

Mike

would not play the piano as a return gesture, and no amount of cajoling, not even when his grip on his own destiny had been loosened by a veritable gush of red wine, would force him to relent.

'I'm not showing myself up,' he said. 'Anyway, you'd lose a fortune, you'd have so many of your customers getting up to leave. I'm doing you a favour. Let's leave it at that.'

It was the usual pattern; Mike recognised, admired and invited to do something that would bring upon himself an attention which he did not wish to have and finding it a struggle to dodge. I remember when I first met him – he was an idol at twenty, pin-pointed with the same sort of worship that later became the right and due of pop stars, but even then he could neither appreciate nor happily accept his fame. His father organised a secretary for him when he was barely out of his teens, to cope with the enormous fan mail, particularly from girls, from all over the world. He was not slow to accept the advantages of his reputation when it came to the heavy attentions of good-looking women, but as for public recognition, that was something he never learned to handle with any comfort.

I first met him at the TT in 1960, when he was staying at Geoff Duke's magnificent country-house hotel halfway between Douglas, the Isle of Man capital, and the airport at Castletown. Straightaway I did *not* like him. But I had mistaken his detached air for one of arrogance, and his shyness at being face to face with a stranger from a national newspaper was something I was not used to finding in someone so famous. Neither, I suppose, could I believe that such a successful youth could be anything other than vain. He had a certain confidence – and who could blame him? – but it was just that. Confidence. Not conceit. And as the week went on and we saw more of each other and grew to understand each other's needs and professional requirements, we became the firmest of friends. I most certainly grew to enjoy writing about his achievements, in which I took immense pride – though I could have done without his father Stan's constant reminders about how brilliant Mike

The Full Genius

was. Those fatherly remarks also gave Mike his deepest moments of embarrassment, but there was no holding Stan when it came to talking about his son's accomplishments, either on the track or off it. It was only with the passing of years that I gradually came to realise just how valuable his father was to Mike. At a time when publicity and hype-merchants were little seen outside film studios, Stan was way ahead of his time in propelling Mike into the forefront of media attention. He worked hard to ensure that the legend was, indeed, furthered, although he could not have succeeded, of course, if Mike had not been the genius he was or as unbeatable as he turned out to be. The two Hailwoods shared that rare quality, a will to win, which found its echoes in Stan's constant chatter about Mike, and Mike's stirring prowess on the track.

It was all a little bewildering for Mike. A hit song, 'Motorcycle Michael' by Jo Ann Campbell, widened his growing fame, teenagers wore 'I Like Mike' lapel badges, and it seemed that every time he parked his white Jaguar saloon there were lipstick messages and phone numbers scrawled on it by adoring girls. He even appeared in the long-running soap opera TV series *Coronation Street* as a tearaway motor-cyclist.

'It was all too much for me to understand,' he said, 'all these birds fancying me. One even wrote to me to say she'd taken Elvis Presley's picture down from her wall after she'd seen me race. And that mine was going up in its place. Then every time I sent any clothes to the laundry or the cleaners they would come back with little notes tucked in the shirt or my underpants or my jackets – the usual thing, a telephone number, a girl's name.'

At a time when media coverage of and interest in motor-cycle racing and its personalities was at a low ebb, Mike's appearance on the scene was a breath of fresh air. His fame, as it turned out, was in his own hands, but he was master of his own destiny only *on* the circuit. *Off* it, Stan made sure, with endless and costly calls and telegrams to the likes of me in the national press, that Mike's success would

Mike

get the right and proper recognition. He was fully justified – by the time he was twenty-one Mike had won more than 200 races and had broken 150 lap and race records.

He had been competing for only four years.

7

Driving Forces

If there are any clues about Mike's self-sufficiency, his fearsome will to win and his single-mindedness in pursuit of excellence, they all trail back to his remarkable relationship with his father, who Mike always called Stan without any of the paternal variations. It would be too glib to say they greeted each other solely on first name terms because they were good friends – they were very much father and son, and I suppose they added to the strength of their love for each other the unusual (certainly in those days) extra dimension of the son calling his father by his Christian name. You could examine the reasons for that until Doomsday and never come up with an answer that would be indisputably accurate. The fact is: I never heard Mike call his father anything other than Stan, or, jokingly, 'Stan the Wallet'.

Stanley Hailwood, a real rough diamond of Northern stock, was the son of a Manchester baker; before he took up the business of selling motor-bikes he made his money by stocking shops with silk ties. He was taken into King's of Oxford as a general manager, but only after he had walked out of the interview.

Having a bad leg, Stan limped quite heavily and when

Mike

Howard King, the shop owner, asked him during the interview if he could kick-start a big 1,000cc machine in the showroom, Stan picked up his bag, closed his diary, put his pen back in his top pocket and made for the door. 'Where are you going?' asked King. 'Don't you want the job?'

And Stan replied: 'It's not a general manager you want, it's somebody to kick over your bloody bikes. And in that case I'm not your man.' His reply so intrigued the boss that he signed Stan right away, and in no time at all the business had grown immensely and soon went public. It was the start of Stan's progress towards becoming a millionaire.

Before the war he had been a racer on grass and at hill climbs, and had even completed, alone, a 24-hour, 500-mile race at Brooklands in an MG. He was that tough. 'He was a real hard case,' said Mike. 'He didn't know how to give up.' It might have been father talking about son.

Mike's elder sister Chris, three years his senior, believes that whatever fighting qualities Mike had were all triggered by Stan's awesome ambitions for his children. 'I was a good swimmer,' she said, 'but that wasn't enough. The old man wanted me to swim the Channel. I'm not kidding. Then when that plan fell away and I was driving a bit, he entered me for the RAC rally.

'Second place was never, *never*, good enough. He wanted only success – a win. He wanted to beat everybody at everything and he wanted us – Mike and me – to beat everybody at whatever he put us in for. He used to make Mike go up on platforms where there was a piano, so he could play and show that he was better than any of the other kids. And Mike hated it, he dreaded being spot-lighted like that. But it was the old man's pride in us that made him do it.

'He was a marvellous father and had great affection for us both, but he did have that drive that was so terrifying. When it hit me, he soon discovered I didn't have the necessary qualities to carry it through; I wasn't beating everybody out of sight in the hill-climbs, the rallies, the car-racing and the swimming. So Mike had to be it. He was the old man's ambition, in full action replay. He wanted Mike to be what he could never be himself, a champion. *The* champion of the

Driving Forces

world. And it was never in any doubt in our family that Mike would be a racer. There was an inevitability about it, with Mike's destiny set by my father.

'He had always organised our lives in such a way that we should benefit in a social and educational sense, to have the advantages he himself was never in a position to enjoy because of his working-class background. He even sent Mike away to boarding-school when he was only six, and it must have been very perplexing and confusing for him. He certainly hated it, even though he was at the same school as me and I was able to look after him a little, although I was only nine myself. I still remember now, all these years later, that it made Mike terribly unhappy and in many ways I think it did him a lot of harm. It set him back.

'What it did do was make him independent. Maybe, at a time when he should have been getting a lot of home and mother's love, he was being starved of that kind of affection – but all the time it was making him a tough little soul who had to rely on his own devices. He sorted out all his own problems, right through life. He rarely turned to anybody else or troubled others with his difficulties, and it all stemmed, I think, from those days when he had nobody except teachers to turn to. I can't imagine how miserable those days at boarding-school must have been for such a tiny little fellow.

'When we were together at home we used to play for hours. We had a beautiful house and our own little tree-island in the middle of a stream at the bottom of our huge garden. And it always seemed to me that we had such fun – but then we got on ever so well and never fought or had the usual brother-sister fall-outs. I think I must have understood how sad he was when he was sent away from home, and I probably wanted to make up for it when we were together in the house at weekends.'

Mike's mother and father had split up, and Stan felt that Mike, in particular, needed the sort of care and upbringing he could not give him at home, but which he would be sure to get in a boarding-school. 'I would guess', said Chris, 'that it was just about the most awful time of little Mike's life.'

Mike

After boarding kindergarten and a spell at Pangbourne Nautical College, an idea given to Stan when he saw Barry, the son of his best friend Chris Bateman, turning out so well, Stan set about moulding Mike to his ideal. A 98cc mini-bike and a 200cc James became Mike's playthings, and on them he tore up the lawn at the family's home in Goring.

The trappings of Stan's business brilliance were all around – the racehorses trained by Steve Donoghue, an RAF Link Trainer flight simulator for Mike to play in, the countryside mansion and the extravagant trips abroad. But none of this was enough for the restless Stan, and he painstakingly set about making Mike into something that he could neither be himself, nor could he make Christine. A champion.

'He really set about it with some determination,' said Chris, 'and after I had been in Canada for four years and came home, Stan had started Mike into racing. I missed his early years, but as it had always been *assumed* in the family that Mike was going to be a racer, like it or not, then it was no surprise at all to me when I returned to England and found we had a wonderboy in our midst.

'The old man would trumpet a bit about Mike's successes and I know it was embarrassing for everybody, but he was only doing what he thought would be good for Mike. And, really, he was way ahead of his time in a public relations sense. There were not many of those sort of fellows around in those days, so Stan voted himself in to do the job. I know it all used to leave Mike blushing, but Stan wouldn't let up. The strange thing – and I'll always remember it – is that Mike told me he didn't think he'd live a long life. He always said, from being about seventeen, that he would die fairly young. It was quite extraordinary, really, and I suppose that is why he always made sure he packed so much into his life while he could. And he certainly did that.

'Being Mike's sister was a tremendous joy. He was always so much fun, so rascally and yet so nice and kind-hearted, but he was shy too, even at home. And that was no act.

'When I look back over the years, at all his staggering achievements, I can picture his face right now, smiling from

Driving Forces

the top of the winner's rostrum at the TT in 1978 when he had won the Formula One race, the first of his comeback. When you have grown up and been so close to somebody for so long, you can interpret their every look, and I can tell you that I had never seen Mike looking so happy and so utterly satisfied, despite his tiredness, than when he turned round and waved to the crowd. His face was a picture. An absolute joy – and I knew deep down just what he was feeling. And, what's more, he had done it all on his own. No Stan to push him. Nobody to force him. He had done it all on his own skill, his determination and a whole deal of bravery. He must have been bursting inside. It really was quite lovely, and it was a sight that I will always treasure in my mind's eye. Special.'

And, indeed, Mike had told me that his greatest sadness was that Stan could not be there to share his jubilation. He had died only a short time before the TT.

'It was as if all those long years ago still had their effect on Mike,' said Chris, 'all those miserable days and nights in boarding-school, all those lonely times, when he had to stand on his own two feet. And there he was, up on that platform, the winner when people had been trying to write him off and say his comeback would never work. They didn't know my Mike.'

Chris Bateman, a family friend who had watched Mike grow up from being a scrawny kid, was another who was not at all surprised by the rise-and-rise of the boy he first set eyes on as a six-week-old. 'Any son of Stan's was bound to be a success, he wouldn't allow anything less,' he said, 'and Mike was plainly destined to go places. And it wasn't merely the man's money that did it; he could have bought Mike the fastest bikes in the world and the boy would still have had to ride them. And once you're out there on the circuit, you're on your own. No dad to help then. At one and the same time, Stan made Mike a winner and the most unpretentious human being I have ever met. I remember him at seventeen. He was racing at Brands and the day was a disaster for him. There were kids all around when Mike rode in, having been blown off, and one said: "Why didn't the bike go? What

Mike

was the matter?" And Mike answered: "It wasn't the bike that wouldn't go, it was me. There was no trouble. Just me, I'm afraid." And I thought that was quite remarkable in a boy so young. No excuses, no conceit. Just an honest answer which underlined his natural reluctance to show off.'

It was only a year later that Stan, in a rage at the Ducati bosses who had fixed up two of their riders with better bikes than Mike's single, had Mike ducking out of sight at the Belgian Grand Prix at Spa. 'Stan was livid,' said Chris Bateman. 'He was creating bloody hell with the mechanics and anybody who was within earshot. There was no stopping him; it was all for the good of his son, but Mike, again, was left monumentally embarrassed. He said to me: "Would you please tell Stan not to do it. I *do* honestly appreciate what he's trying to do for me, but I get so upset when he goes on like that."

'Mike was in awe of his old man, he looked up to him and respected and loved him, but I don't think he always appreciated Stan's blunt and forthright manner. Not when he saw how it affected other people. Stan, on the other hand, wanted only the best of everything, and certainly the best results for his son. Second places were no good to Stan, and he was furious when he couldn't have a win.

'He nearly went up in smoke when he entered his daughter Chris in the RAC rally. All she had to do was finish and she would have won the Ladies Prize; as it was, she turned up half an hour after it was over and lost out on the trophy. Stan was livid. Chris was the only woman entrant and she couldn't possibly miss out on the prize. At least, that's what he thought. I think that is when her rallying career came to a full stop.'

Stan, who once, after deciding that he had not seen enough of America, took his Bentley Continental across the Atlantic and drove it through the (then) forty-nine states, wove a spell over his two children which demanded a winning streak from them both. 'He was the perfectionist,' said Bateman, 'and he could understand only victory. No wonder Mike did turn out to be the best; he was almost forced into it.'

Driving Forces

The cold fact that Mike failed to beat the world when he sought to repeat his bike success in cars frustrated him rather more than he would allow people to realise. The cars, too often, were simply not capable of matching his dash and his undoubted flair. If that might suggest he was a driver without sympathy for his engines, I would assert right away that nothing could be further from the truth. The machinery was not equal to the man; the John Surtees cars and Tim Parnell's all fell short of what Mike demanded at the top level, and I am not alone in believing that, given the right backing, he could have made his mark in Formula One. It was sadly ironic that when he finally earned himself a good drive – with the Yardley-McLaren – it almost cost him his life and most certainly ended his car-race career. Up to the point of his crash in Germany, he had looked like a man who could follow Surtees as the only two- and four-wheel champion of the world. There were enough Grand Prix racers around who viewed Hailwood as a threat to their own reputations, and who saw him as a man with enough pace and talent to link another British championship challenger to the world's greatest, most coveted, racing prize.

The legendary Juan Fangio, staying coincidentally in the same hotel as me in Milan one night, told me: 'That 'Ailwood, 'e's good, very good. And very fast. I think he will do very well in the championship. I like very much the way he drives; but the cars, well, they're not so good. But when he gets a car that is fast enough and does not break down, then I think he make plenty trouble for the others.'

David Hobbs, the one-time Grand Prix driver turned sports-car ace, and friend of Mike's for many years, said: 'Mike was as fast as anybody around and he always said I was a better driver than him, but that was rubbish, and I know he could have gone all the way. He was a brilliant driver and he was brave too. He could neither spell fear, nor did he know what it was. And he loved his time in Formula 5000 – those big beasts used to suit him and the fellas racing them were his sort of crowd. They were not quite as stuffy as the Formula One guys.'

John Surtees had had an eye on Mike's performances in

Mike

Formula 5000 in 1969 and 1970, and he liked what he saw – so much so that despite Mike's growing reputation as a crasher, John reasoned that it must be the equipment and invited him to join the Surtees team. John said later: 'I thought that with his record on bikes, his eyesight, his reactions and his ability, he had to be better than his results suggested. I was looking for a driver for a car I was making, so I got Mike. I had remembered old man Ferrari's idea – you could add safety to fire, but not fire to safety. And what he meant was that people with a real competitive streak in them, which would make them great, could be taught to drive safely, but those without the real fire in their belly in the first place would never reach the heights.'

The Surtees-Hailwood tie-up, certainly in Formula Two if not in the other ratings, was an unqualified success and Mike not only benefited from his hero's expertise in car building at that level, but also learned something of the master's technique and attitude to car racing. And he took the European Formula Two championship title for Surtees in 1972, with men like Nikki Lauda and Ronnie Peterson in his wake.

It was a far cry from the first halting steps Mike had taken in car racing, those uncertain days when he had bought a half share in the Reg Parnell team seven years earlier. Then, the cars were barely competitive. The feeling was that the BRM engine wasn't a good marriage with the Lotus chassis; unreliability and power loss seemed to follow. He had no wages and took a share of the prize money to cover his expenses, and while he was convinced it was a necessary and vital period of his career in cars, he was rarely going faster towards his final ambition than a man marking time. He could have been forgiven for thinking he was on his way after his Formula Junior successes, but perhaps he should have stayed at that level for a little while longer. As it was, Formula One beckoned, and foolishly, then, he answered the call. To his cost. And largely to his embarrassment, because he could not repeat his motor-cycle racing form. It was impossible – the cars would not allow it.

Problem followed problem with Parnell and with Surtees,

Driving Forces

breakdowns and mishaps. After Tim Parnell had taken over from his father Reg, the Lotus 25s were all fitted with BRM V8s – but they could not get Mike first across the line anywhere.

And with Mike mixing cars and bikes together in 1964, he enjoyed roaring success on two wheels and stomach-churning disappointment on four. He retired in the rain at Snetterton, was fifth after starting at the back of the grid at Goodwood, and then was hit by clutch trouble which dropped him into seventh place at Syracuse after he had been third fastest in practice. Aintree saw him run into engine trouble and he was forced to drop out; but then at Monaco, with the car oversteering like a mad thing, he drove bravely into sixth place – his first world championship point, but the last, too, for another seven years. His transmission broke in Holland, and a week later in Belgium he was sick and missed the race. He finished eighth in France after driving all the way from the Dutch TT motor-cycle world championship round. The British Grand Prix, where he really wanted to do well, saw him suffer engine failure again; but in Solitude, despite a bickering ignition snag, he ran into ninth place. He failed on the last lap of the German Grand Prix and, hair-raisingly, at Enna, in the so-called Mediterranean Grand Prix, he had a terrifying skid into a lake.

'It was full of snakes,' he said, 'and I was up to my neck in them. I went for the shore like a bloody torpedo.'

But the trouble went on and on: at Zeltweg, in the Austrian Grand Prix, he was fourth until his suspension collapsed and he fell back to eighth. At Monza he had engine trouble, but Watkins Glen looked as if it might change the Hailwood run of bad luck. He was running fourth, but then an oil pipe broke with only a handful of laps left. An overheating problem saw him off in Mexico – and the whole season's experience, which probably involved him losing all his hard-earned motor-cycle racing winnings just to keep the cars going, left him a bitter, disappointed and frustrated man. The year after, 1965, was not much better – and he sold his share back to Tim Parnell. He was a much chastened

Mike

man, at his lowest ebb, but David Hobbs was near.

It was a friendship, like so many others Mike built up, which started amidst a great deal of uncertainty, but which, after the first tentative probings, was cemented for ever. Hobbs and Mike were teamed up by a Yorkshire businessman who wanted them to drive his Ferrari 250LM in a support race for the South African Grand Prix at Kyalami.

'I wasn't certain,' said Hobbs. 'I'd heard so much about Mike and I had definite misgivings. I didn't think he was a very nice guy. I'd heard so many tales about him from Formula One – he was hard to get on with, he couldn't be bothered with car-racing types, all that stuff. And he wasn't so keen, either. He didn't like the idea of linking up with some Hooray Henry, some car racing Yahoo – me – and it didn't seem like it was going to work out. Of course, when we both got there all this apprehension just went right out of the window and we had an instant rapport, an ability to laugh with each other and have fun, which lasted right until the day he died. We got on like a house on fire.

'We got fourth and then we did the rest of the season down there together. It was a lot of fun. We won a couple of races. We even did a holiday at Lourenço Marques – and that was the best time I've ever had in my life. We had ten days, ten memorable, lovely days on the coast. We did a bit of water-skiing and, of course, Mike, who said he'd never done any, was up on one ski, doing all the tricks and turns and all the fancy stuff. He was very good at it – he had such fine balance. He'd been doing it for ages, but he wouldn't let on. I've still got the film of his antics and it's lovely to see him having such a good time.'

The big rough and tough Hobbs, a man with a fine sense of humour and therefore right up Mike's street, paired up with Hailwood at Le Mans in 1969, where they raced a Ford GT40 for John Wyer. They might have done better than third had they not suffered brake problems. A year later, in a Porsche sponsored again by John Wyer, Mike crashed out of Le Mans when he was running third in the wet on dry-weather tyres.

Mike's on-off romance with cars, a bitter-sweet relationship, only settled into a steady affair when he raced

Driving Forces

five-litre V8 Formula 5000 cars. He loved them. The big Lola he drove was not much of a match for the rather more sophisticated McLaren and Surtees cars, but with him at the helm and determined to salvage something from somewhere in racing cars, he more than made up for its ability to wear out shock absorbers and overheat its tyres. At the same time as he was teamed up with Hobbs in the long-distance sports car events, he was racing against him in Formula 5000.

'I was playing silly buggers on the grid at Brands Hatch,' said Hobbs. 'I was on the second row and ran right over the top of Mike. I managed to take out half the field. I thought it was excruciatingly funny at the time, but nobody else did. And Mike wasn't best pleased – he was quite cross, but he saw the funny side of it later.'

Hobbs's view of the Hailwood style was that he had the ability to be the world champion in cars, he was plenty quick enough, but the story of his life seemed to one of constant breakdowns – few of which were Mike's fault. Even though Mike and John Surtees enjoyed some rapport and a little success, they found themselves at odds quite a few times and, really, it was only Mike's fine sense of loyalty to the former motor-cycle champion that kept him on duty in the Surtees line-up. It had to finish up with a final split – which, in 1973, is precisely what happened.

'After he had fallen out with John and had been drafted into the Yardley-McLaren team, everybody could see his true potential,' said Hobbs, 'but even then the McLaren team was split in two, Marlboro and Yardley, and Marlboro, with Emerson Fittipaldi and Denny Hulme, were getting the best of the deal, the best of the cars, and Mike was left with machinery not quite so good. He always said "I can't drive these bloody Formula One cars," but even when he crashed in Germany he was cracking on for second place against Jackie Ickx and Ronnie Peterson. Peterson for my money was one of the finest Formula One drivers of all time and Ickx was no slouch, but here was Mike, who claimed he couldn't drive Formula One cars, giving them a hot time.

'It was a great tragedy that his career should have ended that way. He was really getting his act together and was

Mike

emerging as a serious threat to all those Formula One twits who were doing it all without the same enjoyment and fun Mike was having. He made an absolute myth of all that nonsense about not drinking before a race – not the same day, but certainly the day before – and the need for celibacy and chastity and abstinence. He proved all that doesn't make a lot of difference. He was very fit, of course, a real tough nut, and it must have maddened some of the guys to see what he was up to when they were having no fun at all and he was still as competitive as the best of them. What with that and his sense of mischief, it's no wonder they couldn't understand him, nor he them.

'I remember when we were racing in South Africa in a long-distance event at Lourenço Marques and I came in to let him take his spell. I had started the session and it was pouring down when I drove into the pits; he was standing there in his civvies. He said, "I'm not driving in the rain, mate," and I had to get back in and carry on. When it dried up a good bit later on, he did take his turn. I was a bit miffed; he was such a bloody good driver in the wet. But we didn't fall out. We never did.'

Mike, talking to a motorsport reporter who had spent most of his time observing a scene of stiff and staid Grand Prix big names, said: 'This is a job, not a bloody religion. I don't think it's necessary to live like a candidate for a monastery. When the race is over I like to get away with a few friends and eat, have a few drinks, and maybe get off to a disco.'

He found willing allies in the likes of Peter Gethin, the famous jockey's son; Paul Hawkins, a larger-than-life Australian with a thirst for fun and action; Dickie Attwood, another racer who took a delightful stand against what was considered to be the established order in Grand Prix driving; Hobbs, of course; and Brian Redman, a Northerner whose accent used to reduce Mike to levels of cruel mockery, but who was very much part of the same style and attitude to life.

There were some wild days when Mike bought a couple of apartments at Heston, near London Airport – parties, film

Driving Forces

shows and comings and goings that must have puzzled the other occupiers to distraction. Mike had more keys cut for friends than there were on the Beefeaters' bunches at the Tower of London – but he was always needled when Nikki Lauda stayed. 'He never bloody well washes up,' said Mike. 'He leaves dirty dishes in the sink and *never* makes his bed.' Mike's stepmother, Pat, used to drive over to Heston from Oxford to clean up the place for him. 'God only knows what she thinks when she sees the mess,' he said. 'I'm going to evict Lauda and his lady. He's got enough money; he can find his own place instead of wrecking mine, the mucky bugger.'

Once Mike had moved into the Heston apartment, the connecting road between there and the city, with the Chiswick fly-over in between, turned into something of a raceway with a variety of cars and race stars driving at hair-raising pace to get to or from another spree. I was with him once in his canary yellow Iso Grifo – later written off when it hit a cow in South Africa – when he got into an enormous heart-stopping slide in the rain and we left the fly-over backwards. By the time I had ducked down behind the dashboard Mike had corrected the problem, with what degree of difficulty I don't know because self-preservation was suddenly uppermost in my mind, but we drove on home as if nothing untoward had happened.

I do not know whether he considered the Chiswick fly-over something of a challenge, but if it stood between him and a date he was likely to be late for – he hated unpunctuality almost as much as he did teetotallers – then it was a problem to be surmounted with all possible speed. And it landed him in trouble with the police in the mid-sixties, at the height of his fame on the world circuits.

He kept pretty quiet about it at the time and years later, when I asked him, he was a little hazy about the details. But what he could recall was that he was fined £75 for dangerous driving, had his licence endorsed and had to pay £25 guineas costs.

It was the only time he ever transgressed – and fell foul of the law, that is – and this time it was his spirits and lateness

Mike

for an appointment which trapped him into trouble. He was flying along the Great West Road towards Chiswick, overtaking cars on the nearside at 75 mph, when the police spotted him. As if that was not enough, when the police moved to overtake in the middle of the fly-over, he drifted outwards to his offside. Mike's E-type Jaguar, with the police looming large in its mirror, was moving quite quickly when the police driver dashed for the gap, but then touched his brakes. The police car walloped the centre strip of carriageway, went bouncing into Mike's car, and shot off the road. Mike carried on, and shortly afterwards left the country to race abroad. He failed to turn up on three occasions to answer the charges. Weeks passed. Mike's lawyer, Peter Crowder, an MP, said Hailwood was not a fugitive from justice; rather he was upholding the prestige of the country abroad. It was lovely stuff, but it failed to stir the patriotic spunk of the justice at Middlesex Sessions, and they issued a warrant for Mike's arrest. The chairman, the Hon Ewen Montagu, was not at all impressed that Mike might have been flying the flag. 'He has a duty to uphold and an example to set other people. Mr Hailwood had best come back, or he may find himself in prison.'

Mike was arrested by Special Branch officers as he left his Lufthansa jet at Heathrow after a long trip from South Africa, via Germany. The globetrotter was home to face the music, and it was headline material. Later he told me: 'I know it wasn't funny at the time, but afterwards it seemed hilarious. It was like Keystone Kops stuff. When I looked in my mirror I could see these two bobbies hanging on to their caps, bouncing about all over the place in that Daimler Dart, an open sports car. Then we touched and they went shooting off. I don't think it did much good to their motor. When it came to court one of the guys, the driver, turned out to be a fan and was nearly as good a witness for me as he was for the prosecution. He said he never felt in any danger during the chase because I seemed to know what I was doing.'

Ten years later all that irresponsibility had evaporated and in 1974 he earned royal reward for his courage – the George Medal – for rescuing Clay Regazzoni. When he found he

Driving Forces

had only half a suit for his Palace date with the Queen – the trousers were in his wardrobe, the jacket forgotten in a Brazilian nightclub, 5,000 miles away – he had to rush from his home, Lindon Hall, to buy a dark suit. It was probably one of the very few times in his life that he ever panicked.

One of those other occasions was when he was caught napping by a young and rising star in Italy, Giacomo Agostini.

'We had not met, but I had been taken into the MV team and given a 500-four for the Italian championships. And I guess it was the usual case of Mike not being worried at all by his opponents in the series. He didn't take it too seriously. He knew he could beat the local riders without too much trouble. And I caught him out in the first meeting at Modena in 1965. I beat him. He was having a holiday, really, I was fighting for my future. I knew all about him and I knew what to expect, so I prepared myself very well and caught him off-guard. It put him in a bit of a panic and I knew I wouldn't have it that way the next time out, at Riccione a week later. He cut out everything to make sure he was fit and ready – no ladies, no drink and plenty of early nights. And this time he got his own back. He took two seconds a lap off me. I had lost the element of surprise and learned that Mike was the greatest.

'We became good friends afterwards and even when he moved on from MV and joined Honda and we had to race hard, we never lost the great feeling we had for each other. The thing that impressed me most about him was his honesty – he would never ride dirty or use nasty tactics. He wanted to win all right, but only on his own strengths and power. And you always knew when you raced him that if you left the tiniest gap, he would be through it – but he never did anything dangerous in all the years I raced with him and against him. He had so much heart and was a very good man.'

Agostini cites the 1967 Senior TT, the one which he lost and Mike won, when they both ran into trouble with their machines, as the greatest race of his life and the one which fills him with regard for his old adversary.

Mike

'It was a fantastic race to be in,' he said. 'Because of the stagger system at the TT we never saw each other at all. We just had to ride as hard as we could, rely on signals, and hope we could motivate ourselves enough to get onto a winning pace without having the sight of the other man ahead, or see him coming from behind. Maybe I would have won if my chain had not broken, but I'm not sure. Remember, Mike's throttle was a problem too. It kept slipping off. But I had to ride harder than I wanted to, faster than was really safe then at the TT. I was hitting the wall with my shoulder at Ballaugh Bridge – the big jump – and I was told Mike was doing the same. I don't suppose anybody who was there will ever forget that one. I won't. And for all sorts of reasons. It was frightening and yet it was exciting. I don't suppose either one of us ever had so many near-misses or spent so much time right over the safety margin for so long, and when you think we were battling over a handful of seconds for six laps – well five in my case – it was tremendous racing.

'But I was even more frightened that night after the race. Mike and I had a big get-together and we got very merry. He was driving me back to the hotel and he spent more time on two wheels than four in his car and round every corner, as we went up the climb to Douglas Head where I was staying, I could see the ocean and it seemed to be right under us half the time. I was sure we'd finish up at least on the beach. But they were mad, mad days. And when you had raced like we had, it was little wonder that we let our hair down.'

It was at a party thrown for Agostini's birthday one June by Sir Dudley Cunliffe-Owen, the boss of the Palace-Casino Hotel, that Mike tricked the Italian racer into a thank-you speech in halting English and prompted him, with a confidentially whispered instruction, to an uproarious obscenity which reduced the luminaries of Isle of Man society to fits at the handsome, winsome, Italian's bloomer.

But it was Sir Dudley himself who reduced Mike and me to tears of laughter in the Isle of Man. He had set up a Rolling Stones concert at just about the time the band was starting to hit the big time, and it was to be staged in the huge dance hall behind the Casino on the promenade in

Driving Forces

Douglas. And Sir Dudley, a stickler for good manners and a former Navy man with a likeable line in pompous reaction, was not sure he had done the right thing. All his fears, he felt, were confirmed when the Stones, who had travelled through the night from Los Angeles via London and had changed jets to get to the Isle of Man, arrived in his hotel to find him as the welcoming committee and me and Mike watching on as curious bystanders.

Mick Jagger, Charlie Watts and Bill Wyman strolled in ahead of Brian Jones and the roadies – scruffy jeans, creased shirts and long hair, and desperately, but desperately tired from their marathon flight. But to Sir Dudley, in his blazer and club tie, short back-and-sides and suede shoes, they were the epitome of everything he frowned upon in men. What's more, they stopped to talk to him – and started scratching their heads and their chests, no doubt from weariness. It was enough to shrink the good baronet back from his bonhomie and say loftily: 'Well, I say, I've paid a thousand pounds for you lot, and I think you're nothing more than a smelly set of bounders.' And 'bounders' became *the* word in the Hailwood-Macauley vocabulary for people to be censured for pretentiousness. Phil Read was a bounder. So was a Manx police sergeant who threw Mike off the trackside at the TT dawn practice because he was not wearing an armband. And so was the manager of one of the labour-intensive works teams, whose ranks of mechanics qualified as a swarm, and whose generally busy attitude and cornering of the market in gold braid on caps and anoraks gave them a slightly Ruritarian glitter which was as ridiculous as it was gaudy.

'But where would we be without these bounders?' said Mike. 'We'd have nobody to laugh at. They take themselves so seriously they just beg to be recognised as figures of fun.' And he smiled: 'Let's go and have a look at Honda. But we don't want to get braid-blindness, so we'll put our sunglasses on.'

If there was an ego to be pricked or a pumped-up, jumped-up fool to be brought down to earth, Mike never shied away; he could be as sharp, as cutting and as

Mike

devastating in his counter-blasts as anybody I knew. Fools were never suffered gladly, and in that he was a replica of his father; so intense was his disregard for those whom he considered to have wronged him, through insufferability or stupidity or sheer dishonesty, that he would wipe them right out of his life. But good friends were locked in for ever, and what they received in return was great affection and a fierce loyalty which transcended everything.

One of the air hostesses on a flight which we took to Daytona in the early 1960s, for what was then the United States Grand Prix, fitted perfectly into the category of 'snobs needing to be brought down to earth'. And there was plenty of time to do the job because the aircraft in which we had crossed from Gatwick to Jacksonville was staying in America until the races were over, and we were due to fly back in it. The stewardess, wary of racing motor-cyclists and with completely the wrong impression of what their status in life should be, tended to be snooty. Her pals were fine, which made the contrast even more wicked, but she could not bring herself to join in or be part of the fun. Three mornings later, with four to go, she awoke to find that her drawers had been rifled and that she had not a pair of undies left. And as she looked across the motel car park towards the reception area, hoping to see the manager, she saw her knickers – nearly every car in the park had a pair tied onto its radio aerial. The knowing smile on Mike's face provided the complete answer. Quite how he had managed to do it, and whether the girl was more friendly than she had led us to believe, I don't know, but Mike's mischief had triumphed. To be fair she appreciated the joke: 'As long as we didn't think it was her way of advertising, she was okay,' said Mike.

It was hardly surprising that the folklore, the legends, very quickly grew around Mike, for when his racing exploits propelled him to the forefront of international recognition the whole picture created was of a man who was everybody's idea of what a professional racer should be. There were, of course, jealousies, people anxious to bring down the precocious kid with an unfathomable line in modesty and an unbeatable streak of skill.

Driving Forces

Even Phil Read, a brilliant rider who had a different sort of forthrightness and an appreciation of his own talent which sometimes did not go down terribly well, would admit: 'I cursed the day Mike came onto the scene. If it hadn't been for him, I would have cleaned up. It was always my bad luck to be around at the same time. I beat him now and then – the first time at Aintree in the Gold Cup when he overshot the final corner – and they were always times to celebrate. But he was always my stumbling block, and I would most assuredly have won more world championships if he had not been in the picture. But having said that, he was a valuable asset to the racing scene; he gave the business a style it had never had before and, maybe, has never had since. He had such a magical quality about him that nobody else had. You knew it could only do good for a sport that needed the lift of men like him.'

In 1981, after Mike had died, I went to the Isle of Man. I walked along the empty grandstand frontage on a wintry afternoon, because somebody had telephoned me at the hotel where we always stayed and said I should go along and take a look. The pit-lane fences had been turned into a touchingly colourful splash of anonymous tributes – flowers and wreaths pinned and nailed to the posts, or placed on the bare wooden seats of the grandstand which had looked down on so many of Mike Hailwood's splendid triumphs. A Manxman who was taping his garland to the pit where Mike had last earned glory – that great Classic race of 1979 – had tears streaming down his cheeks. 'I have never seen anything like this before,' he told me, 'and a lot of good men have been killed racing here. But this shows what love there was for Mike. There was nobody like him.'

He did not realise it, but he was speaking for a whole world.

Index

Agostini, Giacomo, 16, 59, 95, 111, 119, 120-21, 127, 128, 129, 131, 151-2
Agusta, Count, 118, 128
AJS, 118, 122
Anderson, Hugh, 66, 108, 119
Andretti, Mario, 49
Anslow, PC Mike, 25, 27, 32
Attwood, Dickie, 50-3, 76, 82, 93-4, 103, 148

Ballacraine, 96
Ballaugh, 96, 152
Barregarrow, 54
Bateman, Chris, 141-2
Bell, Derek, 16
Benelli, 128-9
Birmingham, 15, 17, 18, 19, 22, 31, 32, 83, 91
Blandford, 106
Braddan Bridge, 11, 12, 44, 78
Brands Hatch, 13, 14, 37, 114, 147
Bray Hill, 67, 86
BRM, 50, 144
Brown, Dr John, 27, 28
Bryans, Ralph, 108, 109-11, 112-13, 114-15
BSA, 122
Buckler, Chris, 11-12, 138-41, 142

Campbell, Donald, 131
Campbell, Sir Malcolm, 131
Carruthers, Kel, 76
Castle Combe, 106
Castletown, IOM, 134
Chadwick, Dave, 106
Cobb, John, 131
Coburn & Hughes, 69
Cooper, John, 127-8
Cooper, Mr and Mrs Peter, 60-1, 62
Creg-ny-Baa, 99
Crosby, Graeme, 87
Crossley, Mr and Mrs Nigel, 57
Cunliffe-Owen, Sir Dudley, Bt, 152-3
Cunningham, Group Captain John, 132-3

Daily Mirror, 60, 71, 100
Davison, Gerald, 58
Daytona, 122-3, 154
Degner, Ernst, 66, 108
Dei, Nardi, 128
Dixon, David, 86
Donington Park, 100, 101, 102, 103, 104
Douglas, IOM, 60, 68, 84, 93, 134, 152

157

Mike

Ducati, 55, 58, 67, 68, 69, 73, 75, 76, 79, 80, 81, 82, 83, 84, 85, 86, 87, 100, 102, 107, 122
Duke, Geoff, 131, 134
Driver, Paddy, 46

EMC, 122

Fangio, Juan, 103, 143
Fisher, Gary, 122
Fittipaldi, Emerson, 48, 147
Fogarty, George, 85
French, Vince, 82
George, Alex, 84, 85-6, 87, 90, 91, 94, 95-7, 99-100, 120
Gethin, Peter, 48, 49, 148
Ginther, Ritchie, 50
Gould, Rod, 20, 83
Grands Prix, cars: Argentine, 47, 49; Austrian, 49, 145; Belgian, 49, 145; Brazilian, 49; British, 145; Dutch, 49, 145; French, 49, 145; Italian, 48, 49, 145; Mediterranean, 145; Monaco, 49, 50, 51, 145; South African, 42, 49, 146; Spanish, 49; US, 145; West German, 35, 44, 47, 49, 145
Grands Prix, motor-cycles: Belgian, 107, 108, 118, 142; Czechoslovakian, 108, 111; Dutch TT, 107, 108, 112, 118, 133; East German, 107, 108, 118; Finnish, 109; French, 107, 108, 112-13, 118; Italian, 107, 108, 116, 118-19, 121; Swedish, 107, 108; Ulster, 107, 108, 110, 118; West German, 107, 108. *See also* Isle of Man TT
Grant, Mick, 60, 62-5, 66, 67, 71, 78, 80, 85, 90-1, 92, 100
Greeba Bridge, 64
Grimshaw, Bob, 31
Gurney, Dan, 103-4

Hailwood, Chris, *see* Buckler, Chris
Hailwood, David, 17, 18, 19, 21, 27, 33-4
Hailwood, Mike (Stanley Michael Bailey), *passim*: childhood, 138-41; early career, 13, 35, 105-8, 134-6; in South Africa, 38-9, 46, 106; marriage and family, 34-40; career 1961-67, 109-22; and brush with police, 149-50; awarded MBE, 131; in New Zealand, 56, 70, 83; business schemes, 20-21, 39-41, 83; career 1967-78, 122, 128-9; car racing, 42, 44, 46, 47-9, 50-3, 129, 143-8; crash at Nürburgring, 35, 44, 47-8, 68, 143, 147; Regazzoni rescue and George Medal, 32, 41-3, 44, 131, 150-1; TT comebacks, 1978 and 1979, 35, 44-5, 53, 54-80 (1978), 81-98 (1979), 122, 129; awarded Segrave Trophy, 131-2; GP and TT wins, 122; accident and death, 12-13, 17-28, 33, 155; funeral, 15-16; memorial service, 11-12; memorials to, 30-1, 155; love of fun, 60-2, 73-4, 97-8, 110, 123, 125-6, 146, 148, 149, 153-4; skill, character and attitudes, 14-15, 34, 41, 44, 45, 46, 50, 51-2, 53, 55-6, 59, 60, 67-8, 71, 73, 76-7, 78-9, 80, 82, 83-4, 87, 88, 89, 91-3, 94, 97, 101, 102-3, 104, 108-9, 110-11, 113-15, 117, 118-19, 120-22, 124-6, 130-1, 132-4, 135, 141-2, 146-7, 148, 150-1, 153-4, 155
Hailwood, Michelle, 12, 15, 16, 17, 19, 21, 22, 23-4, 25, 26, 27, 28, 33, 34
Hailwood, Pauline, 11-12, 15, 16, 17, 19, 25, 26, 28, 29-44, 68, 104
Hailwood, Stan, 35, 105, 106, 115-17, 118, 134, 135, 137-42, 141
Haslam, Ron, 86, 87
Hawkins, Paul, 148

Index

Hennen, Pat, 78, 91
Herron, Tom, 60, 63, 65, 72, 73, 75, 78, 83
Highlander, 31
Hill, Graham, 48, 49, 52
Hillberry, 87
Hobbs, David, 16, 53, 143, 145, 146, 147-8
Hocking, Gary, 118, 119
Honda, 16, 58, 59, 66, 68, 71, 74, 75, 84, 85, 86, 95, 96, 100, 104, 107, 108, 109, 110, 111, 112, 118, 119-20, 121, 122, 129, 130, 131, 133, 151
Hulme, Denny, 46-7, 48, 53, 147
Hunt, James, 16
Ickx, Jackie, 42, 48, 49, 147
Ireland, Dennis, 91
Isle of Man, and IOM TT races, 11, 12-13, 15, 29, 30, 31, 35, 36, 37, 44-5, 53, 54-98, 99, 106-7, 108, 112, 115, 116, 117-18, 120-1, 122, 129, 130, 131, 132, 134, 151, 152, 153, 155
Ivy, Bill, 38, 46, 66, 97, 108, 114, 119, 123

Johnson, Amy, 132

Kawasaki, 71, 78
Kyalami, 42, 48, 49-50, 146

Lauda, Nikki, 144, 149
Le Mans, 50, 53, 93, 133, 146
Lola, 147
Lotus, 50, 144

Mallory Park, 79, 80, 100, 101, 127
Marlboro, 59, 147
Martini, 55, 59, 75-6
Mass, Jochen, 39
McIntyre, Bob, 46
McLaren, 147. See also Yardley-McLaren
Millward, Peter, 18, 31-2
Minter, Derek, 13-14
Mondial, 122

Morris, Mr and Mrs John, 57
Moss, Stirling, 131
MV, 105, 107, 108. 118, 119, 120, 121, 122, 128, 129, 130, 131, 151
MZ, 108, 119, 122
Newman, Paul, 133
Norton, 69, 107, 118, 122
NSU, 107, 122
Nürburgring, 35, 44, 47, 53, 68

O'Dell, PC John, 26-7, 28
Ogborne, Martin, 87, 88, 89, 90, 93
Oulton Park, 69, 105, 106

Pangbourne Nautical College, 113, 140
Parnell, Tim, 143, 144-5
Parnell, Reg, and Parnell racing team, 50, 51, 144, 145
Perris, Frank, 66, 108, 119, 127
Peterson, Ronnie, 48, 144, 147
Pharo, Mr and Mrs Ronald, 22, 23, 24, 25
Phillis, Tom, 118
Postlethwaite, Harvey, 53
Provini, Tarquinio, 107

Ramsey, IOM, 65, 73, 74, 96
Read, Phil, 58, 63, 66-7, 68, 70, 71-2, 73, 74-5, 97, 108, 112, 113, 114, 119, 153, 155
Redman, Brian, 49, 148
Redman, Jim, 53, 66, 97, 108, 109, 111, 112, 114, 118, 119
Regazzoni, Clay, 41-2, 43, 44
Revson, Peter, 48
Rhencullen, 64
Richards, Ian, 73, 75
Robb, Tommy, 108, 119
Roberts, Eddie, 85
Robinson, Roy, 114
Rolling Stones, the, 152-3
Romero, Gene, 122
Ronaldsway, 83
Rutter, Tony, 91, 92

Sawyer, Rod, 17, 18, 19, 20, 27
Sheene, Barry, 45, 87
Shepherd, Alan, 108, 119
Signpost, 99
Silverstone, 62, 122
Slinn, Pat, 81, 85
Smart, Paul, 122
Snaefell, 96
Snetterton, 35-6, 145
Sports Motorcycles, 68, 76
Stewart, Jackie, 41-2, 45-7, 48, 49-50, 131-2
Surtees, John, and Surtees racing team, 16, 47, 143, 144, 147
Suzuki, 78, 83, 84, 87, 90, 91, 92, 95, 96, 109, 127

Taveri, Luigi, 16, 118
Taylor, Jock, 104
Triumph, 122
Tully, John, 39

Ubbiali, Carlo, 107
Union Mills, 84
Warr, Peter, 53
Wheatcroft, Tom, 101-3, 104
White, Rex, 87, 88-9, 90, 94
Whitmore, Raymond, 22, 23, 25, 28
Wilkinson, Mr and Mrs Ken, 57
Williams, Charlie, 63, 86, 87
Williams, John, 63, 72, 73, 75
Williams, Peter, 69
Wolf, Walter, 53
Woodman, Derek, 119
Wyer, John, 53, 146
Wynne, Steve, 68-70, 72, 75, 76, 79-80, 81-2, 85, 100, 104-5

Yamaha, 44, 55, 59, 66, 67, 70, 75, 76, 77, 83, 89, 108, 119, 122
Yardley-McLaren, 47, 143, 147